Stay or

Stay or Move?

Church loyalty

Tony Ling

with Karen Maheson

Harvestime

Published in the United Kingdom by:
Harvestime Services Ltd, 12a North Parade,
Bradford, West Yorkshire BD1 3HT

First published by Harvestime
First printed January 1989

Other versions referred to are: New American Standard Bible (NASB) and Revised Authorised Version (RAV)

British Library Cataloguing in Publication Data

Ling, Tony
Stay or move?
1. Christian church
I. Title II. Maheson, Karen
260

ISBN 0–947714–63–4

Typeset by: Grassroots Ltd, 364a Regents Park Road,
London N3 2LJ
Printed and bound in the United Kingdom by:
Richard Clay Ltd, Bungay, Suffolk.

Contents

Acknowledgement

Grateful thanks to Peter and Jean Wilkinson, who worked hard to gather the real-life stories of moving from one church to another which are an essential part of this book.

Note: The names in these stories have been changed.

Introduction

The most frustrating thing about buying furniture from a do-it-yourself store is that there always seems to be something vital missing from the pack.

Visualising with eager anticipation the fine display of fittings soon to grace your bedroom, you are keen to get started right away. You arrive home with your boxes only to discover that several screws are missing and the instructions are incomplete. Not only that, it's Saturday evening, the shop shuts in five minutes and you had your heart set on moving everything into the new wardrobes tomorrow, if not before!

What do you do? Wait until you can go back to the store and obtain the missing items? Or go ahead anyway, hoping you can still assemble the furniture correctly and that a few missing screws won't make much difference?

Experience shows that to try and assemble furniture without full instructions and a complete kit is likely to result in severe frustration and a good deal of wasted time. Not to mention shelves that wobble and wardrobe doors that refuse to close properly. Yet many of us are trying to build our Christian lives that way.

Some of us start out with enthusiasm, eager to see our town turn to God – by the end of next week if possible! We join a local church only to find that tradition takes priority over God's Word and few share our longing for a closer walk with God.

Disillusioned by the lack of vision in the church, and the restrictions upon our moving forward with God the way he wants, we struggle to keep our own vision alive. Soon, our enthusiasm is replaced by frustration and a sense of failure.

Others of us settle in churches where we hope our desire to learn God's ways and find his will for our lives will be met, only to be confused by critical attitudes and disunity. Our hunger remains unsatisfied. Disappointed by our lack of personal growth, empty and longing to be filled, we cry out, 'There must be more to it than this!'

Still others of us have grown comfortable in our churches, content to maintain the *status quo.* Faintly aware that the Spirit of God is moving today in ways beyond our current experience, we catch an occasional glimpse but quickly settle back, never quite seeing that God wants to bring us into the mainstream of his purpose, use us mightily and bless us abundantly.

Like the do-it-yourself man, we are trying to build our spiritual life without full instructions and a complete kit.

We are struggling to build in an environment where people are willing neither to put the whole Word of God into practice nor to acknowledge the gifts and ministries he has given to enable us to build to his plan. Vision and enthusiasm, though vital, can never be enough on their own – and we find that, spiritually speaking, our wardrobe has an ominous slant.

Perhaps you have experienced something like this yourself. You may even find yourself in a similar situation right now. You have searched for answers but they always seem to elude you.

If that's you, then it's time to go back to the Maker's instructions. It's time to look into the Word of God and take counsel from him.

Each one of us born into the family of God has a unique inheritance to claim and a unique role to play in our Father's house, a role reserved for us alone. So let's not delay any longer. The devil has been robbing us for far too long and it's time to tell him where to get off.

As you read on, may God speak clearly into your situation, leading you into the richness of all that he has already set aside especially for you.

1

What am I doing here?

He watched a herd of pigs, his only companions these days, crowding feet and snouts into the feeding-trough – and almost envied them. Born to greater things, destined for higher service, you can almost hear the tearful whisper as he asked himself, 'What am I doing here?'

He cast his mind back to that morning months ago when he had left the security of his father's house. There had been a sparkle in his eye then, not to mention a bagful of money in his hand. But the money had soon been squandered on short-lived pleasures, of which not even the memory remained to comfort him now.

What a fool he had been! He had turned his back on his father's house, wasted away his inheritance, and ended up in a pigsty.

Shivering in the cold wind, he tried not to think of his room and the place of honour he had enjoyed back home. He had held a position of responsibility in the family business then, putting his God-given gifts and abilities to full use. But now he was reduced to feeding pigs, and his only shelter was a reeking sty.

He longed to fill his empty stomach with the pods the pigs

were eating but doubted he would be able to digest them. If only he had someone to talk to! Maybe it would take his mind off his hunger. But he was alone and he found his mind wandering back to home again and the companionship of his father – a gentle, loving man who had always tried to instruct him in the ways of God. How he wished he had listened to him now.

The turning-point for the Prodigal Son came when he faced up to himself honestly and took the only righteous course of action open to him: he returned home to ask his father's forgiveness. God blessed him for it by fully restoring him to his family.

The Revised Authorised Version describes his realisation of the need for change in the words: 'He came to himself' (Luke 15:17). Stripped of all the externals that had recently made up his life, he was forced to see himself and his situation as they truly were.

And this is where we must begin if we mean business about getting our lives in tune with God and keeping them there.

One preacher said of the Prodigal: 'He took off his coat and came to his shirt. He took off his shirt and came to his vest. Then he took off his vest and *came to himself!*'

We must do something similar, consciously stripping off the layers of tradition and habit that make up our lives. We must look beyond the familiar religious routine and the comforts and securities we have clung to for so long. Weighing very carefully the advice and opinions of others, we must ask ourselves, like the Prodigal Son, 'What am I doing here?'

Then, aware of our tendency to make excuses for ourselves, we must determine to answer that question with complete honesty and, in the light of God's Word, make whatever changes the answer requires.

'Be on guard for yourselves'

The Bible's call to 'be on guard for yourselves' (Acts 20:28 NASB) isn't a call to a life of introspection. It is a call to keep a check on our own lives for the sake of our own well-being – part of an ongoing process designed by God to keep us right in the centre of his will and on the cutting edge of his purpose.

It doesn't matter whether we have been saved for ten years or ten weeks. It doesn't matter whether we hold a position of leadership or not. Self-examination is necessary for us all.

The apostle Paul gave a similar command to his young *protégé*, Timothy. 'Pay close attention to yourself,' he urged (1 Timothy 4:16 NASB). He was concerned with the effectiveness of the young man's ministry – his teaching, preaching, exhorting and use of spiritual gifts – but in the midst of it all he pinpointed a priority on which all the rest depended: 'yourself'.

'But surely it's my pastor who is responsible for my spiritual well-being,' you may reply. 'I take my direction from him.'

True, God has provided spiritual leaders to shepherd us in our faith, and those of us in leadership ourselves need to take our ministry seriously. As those who keep watch over others, we will be called to account to God for the way in which we have led (Hebrews 13:17) and, as teachers, we will incur a stricter judgment for the word we have taught (James 3:1). Nevertheless, those of us who follow leaders and are taught by them are not absolved from responsibility for our own condition. We must one day give *an account for ourselves* (Romans 14:12).

While leaders certainly need our love, respect and co-operation, we must not fall into the trap of relying so heavily upon them that we fail to think for ourselves.

Leadership is no guaranteed safeguard against missing the way in our spiritual pilgrimage – remember the faithless kings of Israel who deliberately led the people astray, and the recurring problem of false prophets throughout Scripture. Remember, too, Jesus' continual confrontation with the hypocritical Pharisees, leaders whom he accused of being 'blind guides. If a blind man leads a blind man, both will fall into a pit' (Matthew 15:14).

The responsibility is ours.

'Examine yourselves,' urges Paul, 'to see whether you are in the faith; test yourselves' (2 Corinthians 13:5). How can we do that? What are the questions we need to ask?

We have already posed the question, 'What am I doing here?' But the experience of the Prodigal Son suggests there are several other matters we need to consider before we can answer that question realistically.

Where am I?

The first thing is to ascertain *where you are now and how that measures up to where you should be.*

Are you truly 'in your Father's house' – a local church where the Word of God is not only preached but put into practice, where God is worshipped in spirit and in truth (John 4:24) and where the Spirit of God moves unhampered? Or are you, like the Prodigal Son, struggling to survive, without vision and without hope, far from home?

One Christian woman, Helen, was in membership with a church for eight years before her disillusionment finally resulted in a decision to leave.

'Basically there was a resistance to the Bible,' she recalls. 'Some, including myself, wanted to go on with God into new and exciting pastures, but others, including the minister, wanted to stay as they had been for years, and they actively opposed the work of the Holy Spirit. Preaching often wasn't put into practice and I knew that, if my hunger for God was to be satisfied, I'd have to move on.'

Richard's experience was similar. 'The church was stuck in its own tradition instead of moving in the way God was prompting,' he says. 'Our minister was born again and baptised in the Spirit, but the church was dividing into those who wanted to go on with God and those who wouldn't accept change. In the end I had to leave and find a people who shared my vision of what God wanted to do.'

Brian's dissatisfaction sprang from the lack of that true worship which he believes is a hallmark of New Testament Christianity (John 4:24).

'There was also a lack of emphasis on certain foundational biblical doctrines,' he adds, 'including water baptism, baptism in the Holy Spirit and the functional role of apostles and prophets. After I attended a Christian conference in 1984, God clearly told me to move to a church which practised these things. It was hard to find myself drifting away from friends but I know I've made the right decision – and I've lost a good deal of frustration!'

How about you? Are you in your Father's house?

What am I doing?

Are you being encouraged to discover, develop and use the gifts and abilities God has given you? Or is that part of your inheritance wasting away, choked by unbelief, prejudice or the fear of others? Are you doing your Father's work in the family business, which is the kingdom of God, or have you been reduced to maintaining a dull and unrewarding *status quo?*

Bob, a church deacon, was training to become a minister. Keenly aware of the new responsibility he was facing and realising his need to be equipped by God, he found his hunger for him growing. In response, he went on a special week of evangelism, during which he received the baptism in the Holy Spirit.

'It was like light flooding in,' he relates, 'and it changed my whole relationship with God. It affected my worship, my prayer life, my understanding of the Bible – it was very exciting!

'On returning to my church, however, I soon realised there was a resistance to the Holy Spirit. The church was heavily weighed down with structure and the leaders wouldn't do anything that might cause opposition. They were preoccupied with holding together what they had, but I had a desire to reach further into God and impact people outside the church. I knew God was trying to build something that wasn't structure-oriented but would touch people's lives.

'Leaving wasn't easy, but it was necessary to enable God to develop and fully use the gift he has placed within me. The greatest satisfaction comes from knowing that I have served God's purposes wholeheartedly and have been able to touch many lives as a result.'

How about you? What are you doing with your gifts and abilities?

What am I feeding on?

Are you feasting at your Father's table on the uncompromising Word of God preached with authority and power? Or are you dieting on a watered-down, wishy-washy version which leaves you as undernourished spiritually as the Prodigal Son would have been physically had he really tried to exist on a diet of pods?

We have all seen pictures of the terrible effects of malnutrition on a human body, but have you ever stopped to think what effect spiritual undernourishment has on your spirit?

Remember Helen, who left to find a church where her hunger for God could be satisfied? Looking back four years later, this is what she has to say: 'If you're not getting spiritual food to satisfy you, then find a place where you will be satisfied – or you'll just shrivel up and die.'

To whom am I joining myself?

Who are the people you have joined yourself to? Are they genuinely and unashamedly born again? Do they love God and his Word? Are they committed to serving his purposes and supporting each other? Are the leaders born again and Spirit-filled, competent and caring?

The sad fact is that many who are born again into the family of God, and whose rightful place is in Father's house, are attempting to join themselves to the unjoinable and to find fellowship with those who, spiritually speaking, are not their fellows. Many unbelievers are pleasant folk, and in everyday life we extend to them all the normal courtesies. But when it comes to local church life there can be no true oneness without each individual's having had a personal encounter with Jesus Christ.

Paul puts it this way: 'Do not be yoked together with unbelievers.' Then he adds a series of penetrating questions, of vital relevance to our church connections: 'What do righteousness and wickedness have in common? Or what fellowship can light have with darkness? What harmony is there between Christ and Belial? What does a believer have in common with an unbeliever? What agreement is there between the temple of God and idols?' (2 Corinthians 6:14-16).

The answer is obvious, and Paul concludes with a powerful call to separation (v17). Obviously we are not talking here about unsaved persons *visiting* the church or even attending fairly regularly. We refer to the situation where unbelievers are accepted as full members, or where the minister or pastor is himself unsaved.

It is inconceivable and unacceptable that genuine believers, righteous in Christ and indwelt by the Holy Spirit, should remain in religious forms and systems where the truth is denied. To do so will lead, in the end, to our own spiritual loss as surely as if we had cast our treasure before swine. Our own eternal foundation may remain secure, but we will have built upon it with materials more in keeping with a farmyard than with a temple (1 Corinthians 3:10-15).

' "Therefore come out from them and be separate," says the Lord' (2 Corinthians 6:17).

2

'What are you doing there?

Jesus was always concerned for the purity of his Father's house. John records his arriving at the temple on one occasion to find his ears assaulted by the non-stop cacophony of sheep, oxen and bartering men and women all struggling to make their own voice heard above everyone else's.

Entering the temple court, he was filled with holy fury as he witnessed the scene inside. After tying some cords together to make a whip, Jesus ran through the court driving out the sheep and oxen and turning over the tables of the money-changers as he went.

'Get out!' he thundered, as men, women and animals fled in all directions. 'Get out! How dare you turn my Father's house into a market!'

His stand for the purity of his Father's house was uncompromising. Hence his forceful response as he witnessed its degradation by people seeking position and prosperity at the hands of gullible worshippers (John 2:13-17).

On this occasion his anger was directed only towards those who had provided the service. He was denying them the use of the temple for their own dubious ends.

But how many of them were willing to listen? Just three years later, unrepentant dealers and an apathetic congregation had made a bad situation even worse. What three years before he had described as a 'market' Jesus now denounced as a 'den of robbers'. And this time he didn't just throw out the sellers; he threw out the buyers as well! (Matthew 21:12-13).

By his action Jesus laid blame on those whose passive acceptance of the defiling of the temple had provided an atmosphere in which corruption could continue to flourish.

It is a subtle form of hypocrisy which allows a person to be appalled by a degenerate religious system and yet continue in it. How can we grumble about the rapid erosion of truth and the ready acceptance of non-biblical practices in our 'church' yet at the same time remain committed to its continuance?

To act in this way is as ridiculous, and as risky, as to live in an old house that is falling down around our ears and never do anything about it. We complain about the leaking roof and grumble about the dry rot. Once in a while we view with consternation the ever-widening cracks in the bathroom ceiling. We become increasingly concerned with the antiquated wiring in the house, which at the best of times is unsafe – yet we never take any active measures to put things right.

Finally, the house falls down one night while we lie sleeping and crushes us in our beds.

Ridiculous, you think? Perhaps, but in the 'church' it is happening all the time – and taking its casualties with it.

'We needed to find life – quick!'

For David and Jean it was recognition that the 'house' was heading for collapse that finally convinced them to move and find somewhere with firm foundations.

'There were several warning signs,' they recall. 'Two successive annual church retreats were led by a godly minister from another area. At the first one he prophesied that God wanted us to open ourselves up to him completely. He implored us to choose life and follow God wholeheartedly. But nothing changed, and when he returned a year later his message was still the same. We hadn't listened the first time around, he said, and he could do nothing but repeat his original message.

'His concern was confirmed by a series of meetings held at the church by another visiting preacher who said, as directly as he could, that something was very wrong with the church and things would have to change. He urged us to shut down all the meetings and seek God.

'We felt very strongly that the church should take his advice. A two-hundred-strong congregation had been reduced by half over a period of two years and numerous families had gone their separate ways, but many just didn't seem willing, or able, to understand what it was all about. Some wanted change and some didn't. Some were for the pastor and some were against him – while he himself just wanted to sit on the fence and please everybody! We were dying on our feet but the environment made change impossible.

'We realised that we desperately needed to find life – and we needed to find it quick!'

Sadly, the church still hasn't changed. The pastor resigned just before David and Jean did, only to be replaced by another who is strongly opposed to the work of the Holy Spirit. So what hope is there for the future?

Such a church, deprived of the vital life of God, is doomed to failure. It may hang on for years as it passes through the various stages of decay, but sooner or later it will collapse – and who is willing to risk being buried under its rubble?

For David and Jean, however, the story is a very different one. They are now in a church where they know the pastor is totally committed to Jesus Christ and they are continually being encouraged in their walk with God. Their own testimony is that they have benefited in every way, but one of their greatest joys was to see their young son give his life to Jesus and get baptised within the first six months of their going to the new church.

In their own words: 'Why settle for less than life? If there's a choice between life and just existing, choose life.'

It's your choice

Christian maturity has a great deal to do with our ability to choose and refuse (see Isaiah 7:14-16; Hebrews 5:14).

From the day Adam sinned and hid himself, the voice of the Lord has been calling, 'Where are you?' He continues to face men and women with his claims upon their lives: 'If anyone comes to me and does not hate his father and mother, his wife and children, his brothers and sisters – yes, even his own life – he cannot be my disciple' (Luke 14:26).

Jesus didn't say that, without the meeting of this condition, it would be *difficult* to be a disciple or that a person would be at a *disadvantage* in his discipleship. Neither did he say that there would merely be a *deficiency* in a person's discipleship. He said, 'He *cannot* be my disciple.'

True discipleship is costly – Jesus left us in no doubt. It requires absolute loyalty to him. Many, like the buyers in the temple, have succumbed to a lesser loyalty, giving first allegiance to a man, a movement, a doctrine or a denomination rather than to Christ. But we do have a choice; if you refuse to buy they cannot sell to you.

Consider Moses. Once the call of God had come to him, he could no longer remain in the comfort of ignorance: 'By faith Moses, when he had grown up, refused to be known as the son of Pharaoh's daughter. He chose to be ill-treated along with the people of God rather than to enjoy the pleasures of sin for a short time. He regarded disgrace for the sake of Christ as of greater value than the treasures of Egypt, because he was looking ahead to his reward' (Hebrews 11:24-26).

There was a choice to make, a destiny to fulfil and a price to pay. He was living among the oppressors of God's people, and God had confronted him with, 'What are you doing there?'

'Well, that was Moses, God's mighty servant,' you reply. 'It's hardly relevant to me.'

Wrong! It is very relevant to you. The details may be different but if you have given your life to God then his call is as much upon you as it was upon Moses. You, too, have a choice to make, a destiny to fulfil and, yes, a price to pay.

All who would choose life and fulfil their calling in God must be prepared to follow him whatever the consequences. Redemption history is well signposted by men and women who remained true and were willing to pay the price.

If you still feel Moses is too great an example for you to follow, consider Elijah. Though he was one of the most mightily used prophets in the history of Israel, James records that he was 'a man just like us' (James 5:17).

Elijah dared to stand alone for what was right among a people who had chosen wrong. In the name of the Lord he confronted sin, compromise and indecision and withstood the religious attitudes of the time.

But, like us, he was human. At the height of his triumph of faith – calling down fire from heaven on Mount Carmel and slaughtering the prophets of Baal – the continued opposition and growing antagonism brought him to despair. Determined now to opt for the quiet life, he ran away and hid in a cave.

But God found him and once again came that searching question: 'What are you doing here, Elijah?' (1 Kings 19:9).

Elijah was simply depressed. He was tired of the opposition. He had tried, but he was alone, the only man zealous for the truth of God. And now, because of his zeal, he was decried as a troublemaker and had become the focus of growing official persecution.

But God had a surprise for him: there were seven thousand others in Israel who had not forsaken the Lord or backslidden into false religion!

As in Elijah's day, there are multitudes of genuine believers in our own generation who remain hidden in the mass of people who pay lip-service to God but have no real faith in Jesus Christ. However, before we grasp a crumb of comfort from that and slip back into complacency, allow me to ask this question: What effect can seven thousand – or seven hundred thousand – have if they are all hiding in caves?

It is time to repent of our self-pity and complacency. The mountain-top of confrontation, not the cave of concealment, is the place for the true servants of God. We are not alone, and God is calling us to stand up for him and be counted.

If you have resigned and retired to your cave, hear him calling, 'What are you doing there?'

3

Where is God in all this?

Going through the motions of Christianity is no more a guarantee of the presence of God than putting on summer clothes is a guarantee of sunshine.

We can dress in shorts and tee-shirt every day and put on sunglasses every time we go out, but if it has decided to rain buckets then rain it will, and there's nothing we can do about it. It's not traditional summer dress that governs the situation but the meteorological conditions at the time. Good weather can never be taken for granted.

Mary, the mother of Jesus, once discovered that his presence cannot be taken for granted. She'd had an uneasy feeling in the pit of her stomach ever since leaving Jerusalem early that morning. At first it had been just a tiny niggle but, as the day drew to a close, it formed itself into a tight knot of anxiety. Something was wrong.

With a sudden shock she realised she hadn't seen her son for several hours – not, in fact, since leaving Jerusalem, when he had been with the rest of the children. Calling anxiously to her husband to help her, she began running through the campsite and soon the whole place was in a turmoil as relatives and friends joined them in the search. But Jesus was nowhere to be found.

At last, fearing greatly for their son's safety, they decided to return to Jerusalem and look for him there. After three days they found him safe and sound in the temple courts.

'Why were you searching for me?' he asked in surprise at their questions. 'Didn't you know I had to be in my Father's house?' (Luke 2:49).

Joseph and Mary had done all the right things. Going to Jerusalem to celebrate the Feast of the Passover, they had been to the right place, at the right time and for the right reasons. They had spent the full length of time there, too – no corner-cutting, no half measures. Surely they could rely on Jesus' presence with them.

They had done everything required of them by law and, leaving Jerusalem, presumed him to be in the caravan. But Jesus wasn't there. He was about his Father's business!

The lesson is obvious: we cannot assume the presence of God just because of what we do and how we do it. We can observe all kinds of rituals and regulations and perform all manner of 'spiritual' obligations, but it is no guarantee that God's presence will be with us.

Mere externals will never guarantee God's approval or oblige him to go along with us and do what we are doing. Even if we have abandoned ritual and regulation in favour of spontaneity in our walk with God, we still can't assume his presence. The real issue is: Are we prepared to go where *God* is going and do what *he* is doing?

Who are you following?

Moses understood this vital principle. Leading the Israelites through the wilderness to the promised land, he said to God, 'If your Presence does not go with us, do not send us up from here. How will anyone know that you are pleased with me and with your people unless you go with us? What else will distinguish me and your people from all the other people on the face of the earth?' (Exodus 33:15-16).

Moses knew there was no point in trying to go somewhere if God wasn't going to be there too. He knew it was the presence of God that made all the difference and guaranteed their success, and he wasn't prepared to go anywhere or do anything if God wasn't with him.

'Well, how do we know when God is with us?' you might ask. 'How does he express his presence with us today?'

Let's have a look at a few personal experiences.

Young Debbie noticed immediately that the people at her new church had a *deep relationship with God* which she hadn't known was possible.

'He was brought into every situation and they treated him like a close friend and Father instead of some far-distant, unreachable being – which had been my previous experience. They didn't sit through the services bored like they did at the old church, singing hymns because that was what they were supposed to do. No, they really worshipped God because they knew him intimately.

'For the first time I experienced the presence of God among his people and it would have been impossible for me to return to my old church after that.'

Laura's experience was similar. The first thing she noticed was the *warm and heartfelt worship* of God. 'And having tasted reality,' she commented, 'we were spoilt for anything else.'

Phil found that at last he had come into contact with a people who *allowed God's Spirit to express the life of God in and through them.* They were letting God transform them into the likeness of his Son. As a result, they were being joined closer together as God strengthened their love for him and for each other and their vision for his kingdom.

They were *seeking God,* both individually and as a body, and the life of God was flowing out of them. They were bringing God's word to the church in *prophecy* (1 Corinthians 14:1, 3) and building each other up with words of *encouragement and exhortation* (1 Thessalonians 5:11). They were *praying for sick people and seeing them recover* (Mark 16:18) and, as a result of their contacts outside the church, *people were being saved* and the church was growing (Mark 16:15).

These features (among others) signal the presence of God among his people. They should be found in any church where the people, instead of turning their hearts away from God, have welcomed him into their lives and invited him to move freely by his Spirit.

The church, you see, isn't an organisation for political agitation or a 'holy huddle' of escapism from the real world. Neither is it history or traditions, doctrines or ministers, buildings or any other temporal thing.

No. The church is *the demonstrated reality of the presence of God.* It is where the risen Christ demonstrates his presence today in word and works.

And that presence can never be assumed; it must be sought out. We can do little about the weather (except put on warmer clothes and carry an umbrella) but we can, and must, do something about the lack of God in our lives. God is longing for a people like Moses who will seek his presence and be willing to follow him.

How about you? Are you following God, or are you expecting him to follow you?

Don't take God for granted

'Well, I know God is here in this church,' some are likely to say. 'I remember a few years back when a number of people got saved at a mission we held and church membership increased quite considerably. God must be with us.'

No doubt he was. But we can never assume God's presence today just because we knew it yesterday.

Look at Samson, one of the great judges of Israel. He was a man who enjoyed outstanding experiences of God. On three occasions Scripture records that 'the Spirit of the Lord came upon him in power' (Judges 14:6, 19; 15:14).

Set apart for God from his birth, he was chosen to begin rescuing the Israelites from the hands of the Philistines. But he abandoned his vow of separation to the Lord in favour of carnal desires, and eventually he was stripped of his supernatural strength. Discovering that the Philistines had once again come to take him prisoner, he said to himself, ' "I'll go out *as before* and shake myself free." But *he did not know that the Lord had left him'* (Judges 16:20).

What a tragedy that one so mightily used in the past was left just going through the motions!

Another great calamity in Israel's history was the day the Ark of the Covenant was taken captive by the Philistines. The Ark was the symbol of God's covenant with his people and the army of Israel had taken it with them into battle, believing its presence would guarantee them victory.

But the hearts of the people had already turned from obeying God, so he had withdrawn from them – and the external symbol of his presence was no substitute.

After a bloody defeat, the wife of one of the priests who had carried the Ark into battle, hearing of her husband's death and the capture of the Ark, immediately went into labour. As death began to close her own eyes she gave birth to a son whom she named Ichabod (meaning 'No glory'), saying, 'The glory has departed from Israel' (1 Samuel 4:21).

The glory of the Lord had indeed gone. God's presence had vanished because his people had turned their hearts from him. And that's not just a fault of past generations. As one woman commented, explaining her move from a dead church, 'I wanted to go where God was *now,* not where he'd been years before.'

The cocoon left behind when a chrysalis emerges as a beautiful butterfly is no more than an empty shell, the dead relic of a past era. There was life in it once, but no longer. And there is no point in clinging on to the cocoon in the hope that the butterfly will return to it. It can't. Life has developed and the old form can no longer contain it.

So it is with God. The life of God is a dynamic, moving force and as God forges ahead with the outworking of his purposes on earth, he expects us to move with him. But we can't do it unless we let go of the empty shell of mere outward religion and seek the fresh and powerful presence of God.

There are many religious establishments today over which is written the word 'Ichabod'. The 'Philistines' of unbelief have stolen and abused the truth of God, and the Lord has departed. Like the unrepentant church at Ephesus, their lampstand has been removed (Revelation 2:4-5).

The ceremony and ritual, tradition and liturgy, religious practice and observance may continue, but the crucial question remains, 'Where is *God* in all this?'

4

Whose church is it anyway?

I once heard about a young boy with a flair for model-making. He spent many long and careful hours designing and building a sailing-boat which, with great pride, he eventually launched on the local pond. With a thrill he watched the wind catch the sails and send his creation racing free across the water.

But his joy soon turned to concern, and then anguish, as he witnessed its headlong rush towards the reed-bed in the middle of the pond. Stuck fast, out of depth and beyond reach, his boat seemed lost for ever and the little boy returned home brokenhearted.

Some days later, passing a junk shop in town, his eye was suddenly caught by the familiar lines of the boat he had made. There, displayed prominently in the shop window, was his very own creation! It bore a price tag now – one which demanded every penny he possessed. Without a moment's hesitation he ran home, snatched up all that he had and returned with joy to purchase what was already his own.

As he stood outside the shop, holding his beloved boat in his hands once more, he was heard to exclaim, 'I made you and now I've bought you. You're mine twice over!'

Bought at a price

As Christians, we too are God's twice over. Can you imagine the tender love with which he created us, a people to be his very own, and the deep anguish he must have felt as we turned our backs on him and plunged headlong to our own destruction?

But his love outshone the disappointment and rejection he must have felt, and he determined to bring us back to himself: 'God so loved the world that he gave his one and only Son, that whoever believes in him shall not perish but have eternal life' (John 3:16).

It is a vast, world-embracing love, but Paul focused it, undiminished in its intensity, upon the individual when he said, 'The Son of God. . . loved *me,* and delivered himself up for *me'* (Galatians 2:20 NASB). That applies to you, too. The Son of God loves you and delivered himself up for you. He chose to redeem each one of us individually, to buy us back even though, like the little boy with the sailing-boat, it cost him everything he had.

All this has a bearing on the church-related questions we have faced in the previous chapters: Where am I? What am I doing here? What does God require of me? Am I really experiencing the power and presence of God in my church situation?

Why should we bother with such questions?

That it's for our own benefit is clear – but it goes far beyond that. God's love, which motivated our redemption, is not just emotion or easy-going affection. Its expression in redemption implies a *claim to ownership.*

In everyday terms, redemption means to recover ownership at a price, just as you recover the title deeds to a house when you have paid off a loan secured upon it. Its explanation in Scripture is similar: 'You are not your own; you were bought at a price' (1 Corinthians 6:19-20).

God bought us back from the power of sin and death with nothing less than the precious blood of the Lord Jesus Christ

(1 Peter 1:18-19). We belong to him. In the light of such demonstrated love, and the righteous demand of loyalty to Jesus which naturally follows, how can we even entertain the thought of trying to live for ourselves? On the contrary, we must be willing to say, like Paul, that whether we live or die we belong to the Lord (Romans 14:7-8).

King David said, 'The earth is the Lord's, and everything in it, the world, and all who live in it' (Psalm 24:1). Everything belongs to God, but that is doubly true of the Christian, who not only belongs to God by creation but has now been bought back by redemption.

He made us and he bought us. We are his twice over.

A chosen people

The Bible tells us that God is concerned with 'taking from the Gentiles a people for himself' (Acts 15:14) – 'a chosen people, a royal priesthood, a holy nation, a people belonging to God' (1 Peter 2:9).

You may have been thrilled by the love of Jesus for the world (John 3:16) and by his love for you as an individual (Galatians 2:20). But are you also thrilled, or even remotely touched, by the glorious truth that 'Christ loved *the church* and gave himself up for her to make her holy, cleansing her by the washing with water through the word, and to present her to himself as a radiant church, without stain or wrinkle or any other blemish, but holy and blameless' (Ephesians 5:25-27)?

Jesus died for the church. Not our church, but his church, a church exclusively possessed by him and one whose loyalty, like that of a wife to a husband, should be to no other.

The church cannot belong to a nation, being shackled to the state, to a practice, a doctrine or an administration. Neither can it belong to an experience or an ideal. No, it belongs to God. It is 'the church of God, which he bought with his own blood' (Acts 20:28).

Why is it, then, that while we seem ready to accept the claims of Jesus upon our individual lives, we also seem prepared to accept the glaring discrepancies within our 'church' lives?

The truth is, if we don't allow Christ to rule 'in church' then we aren't really allowing him to rule us as individuals either. To quote a well-known saying, 'If he isn't Lord of all, then he isn't Lord at all.'

Built to a pattern

Knowing that the church belongs to God, can you really believe that he who paid such a price to possess it should then abandon it to its own devices, especially as far as its structure is concerned?

That would be like a man spending a fortune on building materials and labour to build the house of his dreams only to allow the workmen to do their own thing and end up with something more like a warehouse than the luxury residence he had set his heart on.

No. Jesus said, 'I will build my church' (Matthew 16:18), and the Bible repeatedly demonstrates that he is intimately concerned with how his church should be.

The book of Exodus contains several chapters on the building of the tabernacle by the Israelites in the wilderness. After giving detailed instructions about every part of its construction and contents, God warned Moses, 'See that you make them according to the pattern shown you on the mountain' (Exodus 25:40). This command, quoted in Hebrews 8:5 and again in Acts 7:44, contains an important principle: *The place of God's presence must be built to God's plan.*

The same was true of the great temple built by Solomon. His father, King David, had intended to build the temple himself but had been instructed by God to leave it for his future son. However, the Lord gave David precise plans for its construction which he was later to pass on to Solomon. ' "All this," David said, "I have in writing from the hand of the Lord upon me, and he gave me understanding in all the details of the plan" ' (1 Chronicles 28:19).

Again, Ezekiel has four long chapters (40-43) describing his revelation 'in visions of God' of an ideal and glorious temple. God's commission to the prophet was, 'Describe the temple to the people....Let them consider the plan, and...make known to them the design....Write these down before them so that they may be faithful to its design and follow all its regulations' (Ezekiel 43:10-11).

God has already prepared a design for us to follow in the church. The question is, are we following it? Are you following it?

Remember the do-it-yourself man who failed to look at the instructions properly and ended up with distorted furniture? It wasn't that he failed to consult the instructions at all, just that he was too busy getting on with what he thought was right to take the time and trouble to obtain the full instructions and find out what he should have been doing.

Let's avoid making the same mistake; God isn't looking for a distorted church.

Remember, too, that although Christ has called us as individuals he has also called us as a body. We are a chosen people, and as a people we must build together. Not just one do-it-yourself man following a set of directions alone, but a group of people, one in heart and mind, building to one precise and complete set of instructions – the Word of God.

No longer living in the shadow

The past is often a shadow of the future. The first television broadcast was just a shadow of the day when pin-sharp pictures would be transmitted live across the world by satellite. The first time an aircraft lifted off the ground under its own power hinted at a day to come when people would be able to travel from London to New York in under four hours – a distance of some three and a half thousand miles.

The previous was a glimpse of the now, and, as the writer

to the Hebrews tells us, it is no different with the things of God. Referring to the Levitical priesthood, he writes: 'There are already men who offer the gifts prescribed by the law. They serve at a sanctuary that is a copy and shadow of what is in heaven. This is why Moses was warned when he was about to build the tabernacle, "See to it that you make everything according to the pattern shown you on the mountain" ' (Hebrews 8:4-5).

The Old Testament tabernacle and temple were merely copies and shadows of things to emerge in the future. They were built to provide hints and shadowy glimpses of better things in store.

As Christians we are now living in that future. We no longer live in the deep shadows of religious mystery but in the direct sunlight of God's purpose and love. Everything pictured and prophesied in the Old Testament becomes a reality for us, 'for everything that was written in the past was written to teach us' (Romans 15:4). The previous was a glimpse of God's 'now' plan.

We understand now that God does not live in a building (Acts 7:48) and that no bricks-and-mortar edifice can properly be called the house of God. Architectural grandeur and extravagant décor in our meeting-places is totally irrelevant as far as the presence of God is concerned. The New Testament conceives the temple of God, not as an inanimate structure made *by* people, but as a living structure made *of* people, the people of God: 'God's temple is sacred, and you are that temple' (1 Corinthians 3:17).

Peter describes it like this: 'You also, like living stones, are being built into a spiritual house' (1 Peter 2:5). And Paul declares: 'You are no longer strangers and aliens, but you are fellow-citizens with the saints, and are of God's household, having been built upon the foundation of the apostles and prophets, Christ Jesus himself being the corner stone, in whom the whole building, being fitted together is growing into a holy temple in the Lord; in whom you also are being built together into a dwelling of God in the Spirit' (Ephesians 2:19-22 NASB).

We, the body of Christian believers – not the place where

we meet – are Christ's church. And even from the few verses just quoted something of a building plan begins to emerge for this spiritual house made with living stones.

It is 'built upon' a foundation, indicating that it is to have an unshakable stability.

It is 'built together', joined stone to stone, displaying its unbreakable community.

It is 'built . . . into', declaring that it has an ultimate destiny.

Yes, God does have a plan. And as a people belonging to Christ, individually and as a body, what will our response to it be? Will we allow God to implement it in our lives or will we stand in his way?

Do you remember Bob, the former church deacon who left his church and his emerging ministry to find a place where he could build to God's design? Before that he was already building. He was already zealous for God. But he wasn't building the house God desired.

How about you?

5

Brought to perfection

A well-tended garden is a visual delight, especially during the summer.

Few gardens can compare with those in the grounds of large country houses. Velvet lawns, soft and springy underfoot, dotted here and there with trees and bushes of every kind. Vivid displays of flowers of endless colour and variety, their blended fragrances filling the air. Neat rockeries and cool refreshing fountains – everywhere a feast of colour, variety and beauty!

Over the years the gardener has worked long and hard to produce such satisfying results: breaking the hard ground and pulling up thorns and thistles; fertilising barren soil; planting, seeding and laying turf – all that goes into turning uncultivated land into a display of nature at its loveliest.

When a dedicated gardener goes into a new garden, he goes in with a sense of purpose. He doesn't just pull up a few weeds here and there and indiscriminately put in a few plants. First he takes a long, hard look at the garden to see where and how best it can be improved. Then he takes time to find and remove every weed and consider which plants to grow, and where. His goal is the perfect garden and he carefully plans the best way to reach that goal.

We, the church, are God's garden. And God, like the gardener, has both a goal for us and a plan to bring it through to completion. As we saw in the last chapter the church is 'built . . . into' indicating that it has an ultimate destiny to fulfil.

God's destiny for his people is a perfect church. We are to manifest the nature and glory of God in the same way as a garden reflects the gardener and, right now, our Father is at work in you and me, pruning and cutting, planting and sowing, removing the rubbish and replacing it with the life of God.

'No spot or wrinkle'

Summing up his ministry, Paul said: 'We proclaim *Christ*, admonishing and teaching everyone with all wisdom, so that we may present everyone perfect in Christ' (Colossians 1:28).

Paul was stating Jesus' declared objective for the whole church: 'That he might present to himself the church in all her glory, having no spot or wrinkle or any such thing; but that she should be holy and blameless' (Ephesians 5:27 NASB).

The illustration this time is that of a wedding. The church Jesus is preparing is to be a flawless bride – 'no spot'. Spots are the plague and embarrassment of adolescence, that formative time before full maturity. But the church of Jesus Christ will be done with all her 'growing pains' and be cleansed from every blemish as she responds to what Paul describes as 'the washing with water through the word' (Ephesians 5:26).

We need to soak ourselves in God's Word, the Bible, allowing it to wash us inside and out. We need to read the Word, hear the Word and study the Word continually. That is the basis of the 'admonishing and teaching' which Paul speaks of as being so necessary. As we respond to it in obedience, the Word will cleanse us and bring us to full maturity.

The church is also to be one in which there is 'no . . . wrinkle'. Wrinkles are the marks of years of care on a face that has seen better days. However honourable, they are a visible testimony of old age. But the church Jesus presents to himself will not be 'over the hill' and on the decline. Like the garden in summertime or a splendid new building, she will be in the prime of her glory – the very perfection of spiritual beauty.

To enable the church to become that perfect building, however, an examination of its foundations is necessary, because only what has been properly founded can be gloriously finished. A detailed study of essential spiritual foundations is beyond the scope of this book,[1] but let's quickly review the basic scriptural requirements.

Washed with the word

The ongoing ministry of Jesus towards his church, carried out by his servants since his ascension, is that of applying God's word to all areas of our life. That 'word' is the whole of God's purpose as revealed in the Scriptures, and it is revealed not only for our interest but also for our implementation. It isn't sufficient just to hear the word; it must be acted upon.

Jesus made that 'action' principle quite clear in the parable of the two builders recorded in Matthew 7:24-27. The wise man who put the words of Jesus into practice was like someone building his house on solid rock with the result that, when the fierce winds and the rains came, all that he had built stood firm.

The foolish man, however, heard the words of Jesus but did not carry them out. With no foundations for his life, when the winds and the rains came, all he had built was washed away. Like the do-it-yourself man, he had built without instructions and it had ended in disaster.

What was true of him is true of any church which builds without reference to the whole counsel of God – or tries to replace that counsel with its own preferences or traditions. Somewhere down the line it is destined to fall, and what have been supposed to be bastions of history will prove to be nothing more than the sands of time – a very shaky foundation.

There is invariably a cost involved, but applying God's Word is a priority, and we must give it priority whatever that cost may be.

For almost thirty years Kenneth had been a member of a denominational church where the pastor was both born again and Spirit-filled. Kenneth himself was baptised in the Holy Spirit while attending that church. It was after being given some leadership responsibility that he found himself becoming more and more convinced of the need to put God's Word into practice.

'I decided to go all out to obey the Scriptures,' he says, 'but this caused much dissension and aggression among members of the church – both local and in the circuit.

'Eventually, some members said I should accept the denominational tradition or leave. Others asked me to stay on but not be dogmatic about the Scriptures, but I knew there could be no room for compromise. My desire was to obey the Scriptures and the Lord fully, and be in a place where the personal and corporate commitment required by the Lord – and necessary for me to grow as a Christian – would be possible.

'Leaving wasn't easy. I had been in the church for a very long time. My family made the move with me, out of deference to me and to the Lord, and found the first year at the new church very difficult. Also, from having a position of leadership I now had no church responsibility at all.

'But God didn't let us down. The encouragement of the people around us and the very positive teaching of the Scriptures has resulted in each one of us growing in maturity. My family are now very happy, entering into the life of the church fully and building close relationships. I know the peace of God in my life and am now able to contribute much more to the life of the church.'

For Kenneth and his family there was a price to pay but they were willing to pay it. And as they put their trust in God's Word he honoured them for it, pouring out his blessing upon them as individuals and as a family.

Is God's Word the deciding factor in your life?

Built on the cornerstone

'No-one can lay any foundation other than the one already laid, which is Jesus Christ,' declares Paul (1 Corinthians 3:11). And to this he adds that the church is 'built on the foundation of the apostles and prophets, with Christ Jesus himself as the chief cornerstone' (Ephesians 2:20).

Paul was saying that the ministries of apostles and prophets are the foundations of the church. These ministries, rooted firmly in Christ and held together by him, are extensions of Jesus himself, who is the mainstay of the whole structure.

We are discovering that right foundations are essential for the fulfilment of God's purpose for his church and the success of our individual lives. If the church is to come to perfection, therefore, apostles and prophets, along with other biblical ministries, must be recognised by the church – and received by her as the appointed and anointed servants of the Lord.

Sadly, many aren't willing to accept apostles and prophets in the church today. They accept that they had a place in the early church of the New Testament but believe they are now no longer needed.

But look at what the Word of God has to say: 'He. . .gave some to be apostles, some to be prophets, some to be evangelists, and some to be pastors and teachers, to prepare God's people for works of service, so that the body of Christ may be built up *until* we all reach unity in the faith and in the knowledge of the Son of God and become mature, attaining to the whole measure of the fulness of Christ' (Ephesians 4:11-13).

God's purpose in giving such ministries to the church is clear from this scripture, and until that purpose is completed God will continue to use them.

They exist – apostles and prophets included – to plant churches, to envision and direct us, teaching us the ways of God. They are men with a God-given understanding of what the Lord wants in his church. Men able to see clearly how God is wanting to work out his purposes and willing to work obediently to put into effect what God is showing them. Men willing to bring the clear word of God to the church – as necessary for us today as it was in Isaiah's day, when God spoke judgment and restoration through the mouth of his obedient servant.

Sean, a pastor, recognised the need in his church for ministry from outside. He didn't like the word 'apostle', however, thinking it presumptuous for anyone to take on such a title. But he had no problem with the functional role of such a person – and indeed welcomed it. Eventually he linked in with a network of related Christian churches which recognised and incorporated all of the ministries described in Ephesians 4.

'The practical benefits are immense,' Sean commented. 'It puts you in touch with people who have a national and international perspective of what God is doing among his people. And it puts you in touch with other churches who share the same vision as you do, which is a great source of encouragement.

'It also gives you access to leaders with special teaching and inspirational abilities and to people experienced in church planting and church growth, helping you to avoid pitfalls and all kinds of potential hazards. Where local leadership is concerned, I believe you need outside help to appoint or confirm appointments and provide advice and help. This takes pressure off the local elders, especially newly-appointed ones, as it provides a court to whom appeal can be made should problems arise.

'I no longer have a problem with recognising a man as an apostle and calling him one. God has said it in his Word and, as far as I'm concerned, that settles it. But I've also been able to appreciate the wisdom of God in it all and see for myself many of the benefits of putting that wisdom into practice.'

What an encouraging testimony from someone who, despite initial doubts, discovered for himself the wisdom of God's ways! Having discovered it, he allowed it to become part of his life, experiencing the blessing of God through his obedience to it.

'On to maturity'

The letter to the Hebrews highlights another aspect of spiritual foundations: 'Let us leave the elementary teachings about Christ and go on to maturity, not laying again the foundation of repentance from acts that lead to death, and of faith in God, instruction about baptisms, the laying on of hands, the resurrection of the dead, and eternal judgment' (Hebrews 6:1-2).

Taking this in conjunction with the scriptures already considered, we conclude that our foundations are to be: first, Jesus Christ himself – a living experience of him in our lives and our meetings and his Word a priority in our life; second, the ongoing input of apostles and prophets; and, third, an embracing of the basic doctrines of repentance, faith, baptism in water and in the Holy Spirit, living in the power of Jesus' resurrection life and living under God's eternal government.

As we have already seen in various testimonies, it is within our own power to place ourselves in the environment which enables these conditions to exist and be exercised. We have a solemn responsibility to live out our immediate (that is, our day-to-day lives here and now) in the light of our ultimate (what God has said we will be). In other words, what we will be, we must now diligently begin to be.

How does this affect us as individuals? Well, here's how Scripture describes our final glorious state: 'Dear friends, now we are children of God, and what we will be has not yet been made known. But we know that when he appears, we shall be like him, for we shall see him as he is' (1 John 3:2).

We are going to be like Jesus. What a glorious expectation! To return to the gardening image with which this chapter began, our waste ground, our hard and barren soil covered with weeds and brambles is being transformed into a fertile, fruitful, beautiful garden. What a promise, and what a hope!

But *we aren't just to sit back and wait for it to happen.* We are to work towards it here and now: 'Everyone who has this hope in him purifies *himself,* just as [Jesus] is pure' (1 John 3:3).

By faith we begin to co-operate with God and implement the word of our expectation into the working out of our experience. If I am to be like Jesus one day then I'm going to begin today.

The same attitude must also be found in the church. We have repeatedly quoted Paul's words about Christ's love for his church. Set in the context of a marriage relationship, Jesus is seen anticipating a glorious completion to redemption history when he presents the church, his bride, to himself. John, however, gives us a glimpse of this process from a different perspective: 'The wedding of the Lamb has come, and *the bride has made herself ready*' (Revelation 19:7).

The church of Jesus Christ should be a pilgrim community, not locked nostalgically into the past, nor wandering aimlessly in the present, but moving with determination to embrace all the purposes of God, actively working with him to become all that he has destined her to be.

Beautiful garden or compost heap? The choice is ours.

Chapter 5 NOTES

1 A helpful guide on this topic is *Essential Foundations,* by Hugh Thompson (Harvestime/School of the Word)

6

You in your small corner?

That God's chosen plan for his church is far removed from what is actually taking place is beyond dispute. But that doesn't mean we have to settle for second best or consider the perfect to be for ever unreachable.

God is constantly giving evidence of the choices he himself has made. Whether it be the raising up of a leader or of a nation, the decisions of the Lord are irresistible. What he has purposed he will perform. All that he intends for his church will be fulfilled. Jesus prayed for it. God planned for it. It *will* happen.

What a source of confidence that is for us! It means that since God has planned for a church without spot or wrinkle, that is what we will be. But, as we have seen, we ourselves have a vital role to play in bringing it about.

How easy it is to bury our heads in the sand. How conveniently we can avoid the cost of making a difficult decision by remaining seated in our own small corners, refusing to listen to, or look at, the reality of what is going on around us.

One church

It only takes a quick glance at Christianity in Britain to see that the church is paralysed by tradition, apathy, ambition, complacency, lethargy and fear of change. Much of this has already been illustrated by the testimonies in this book.

One symptom of the paralysis is division – the result of a reluctance to move forward with God's unfolding purpose. But it was never God's plan for the church to be fragmented. His plan has always been for one church – for one body of people united in him through his Son, Jesus Christ.

That's why the New Testament church, fresh in the excitement of this revelation, couldn't come to terms for a moment with the idea of a fragmented body. The council at Jerusalem, described in Acts 15, reflected the growing tensions between the 'legalists' and the 'liberated'. But overriding all the differences was a strong determination not to polarise into Jewish and Gentile denominations.

As Paul tells us in Ephesians 2, God has made from such naturally prejudiced and segregated companies 'one new man' (v5), having removed all the barriers between them by the blood of Jesus. He had no plans for separate Jewish and Gentile churches, Greek and barbarian churches, free and slave churches. God decided on one church.

So where are we going wrong?

Many have sought comfort in the idea that our historical and traditional differences are really parts of the whole. All too often the church has tried to spiritualise its way out of its dilemmas and discrepancies by smugly declaring, 'We are one – in the Spirit.'

But that does nothing for those of us who know, in the depths of our hearts, that our differences are not so much facets of the whole as broken fragments – with sharp, jagged edges.

We may be one in the Spirit, but the prayer of Jesus for the unity of his church is 'that the world may know' (John 17:23 NASB), and people outside the church cannot understand the spiritual concepts with which we ourselves are so familiar (see 1 Corinthians 2:13-16). So none of our pious attitudes can excuse us from being anything other than what we ought to be.

Nevertheless we have an uncanny ability to turn our spiritual failings into religious virtues. Human traditions have rapidly become taught as the doctrines of God, and it is amazing how many people who truly love the Word of God have had their minds blurred with all kinds of non-biblical concepts.

It's time to get behind the façade and see the reality. We cannot just accept all that we hear. We must first judge it by the Word of God.

Some spiritual misconceptions

I can remember, in my own Christian experience, being presented with ideas which sounded spiritually plausible at the time but somehow would not sit easily in my heart.

Within a few weeks of being born again, fired up with zeal to win the whole world for Jesus, I was taken in hand by one of our church leaders. This man, held in great awe in our fellowship, took me aside to explain the principles of evangelism to me.

'It is nothing more than one starving man telling another starving man where to find bread,' he explained.

In the zeal of my immaturity, my mental reaction was, 'That can't be right.' Now, after years of walking with God, learning his ways and growing in wisdom and understanding, I *know* it isn't right.

Evangelism must be one well-fed, satisfied person calling starving people to come and eat. A person lacks credibility if, while claiming to know where food is, he or she continues to display all the symptoms of malnutrition. The Christian must be able to say to the world, 'What I *have* I give you' (Acts 3:6).

Some years later, when I embarked on full-time ministry, I was confronted with some major decisions. An older man with whom I worked at that time counselled me on an infallible way of discerning the will of God for my life.

'I always know when I'm in the will of God,' he told me. 'It's when I'm doing what I don't really want to do.'

I was horrified. But most of us have probably come across this misconception at some stage in our Christian walk. We allow ourselves to believe the lie that God's will for us cannot possibly match up with what we really want to do.

Fortunately for me, I had already learned from Scripture that the will of God is 'good, pleasing and perfect' (Romans 12:2), and could better identify with David when he testified, 'I *delight* to do thy will, O my God' (Psalm 40:8 NASB).

Distorted reflections

Another great spiritual misconception was propagated by one of the brighter men who studied with me at Bible school. His student career had been a long one. Having won distinction at school, he had gone to university to obtain his degree, and then to college to gain his teaching diploma.

And now, here he was at Bible school with more letters after his name than I had *in* mine! For me, never having attained much at school, such learning was awe-inspiring. Surely, I thought, every opinion he expressed must carry the stamp of divine approval.

However, the clay feet of this intellectual giant were exposed and my idol fell one day when we were discussing the grace of God. Divine grace was wonderfully expressed, he believed, in the provision the Lord had made to accommodate man's diverse backgrounds and personalities.

His theology unfolded something like this. The Anglican Church, he said, had been specifically provided for the cultured upper classes whom he believed were generally more inclined towards respectful, religious solemnity, while the middle classes, he believed, would be more at home in a Baptist, or some other nonconformist, non-liturgical establishment.

Continuing in the same vein, he methodically worked his way

down through the religious denominations and social strata of western civilisation, ending up somewhere near the Salvation Army!

What a shock! But while it is patently ridiculous, it does highlight our natural human tendency to try to recreate God in our own image and conform him to our own likeness.

Often our mental image of God has come about as a result of human thoughts and suggestions picked up from various sources. Receiving them as truth, we fail to check whether they are an accurate reflection of God as he is revealed through his Word and in his Son, Jesus. And instead of seeing God as he really is, all we see is a distortion.

Just as looking at yourself in those convex and concave mirrors you find at funfairs gives you a grossly distorted picture of what you really look like, so we can find ourselves looking at a gross caricature of the real God. When that happens, our thinking, our doctrine and what we have built also become distorted.

We aren't necessarily way off track. It may just be in one or two small areas that we aren't seeing God clearly. But whatever the degree of distortion, there is only one answer: go back to the Word of God, the true mirror, and see what God has said about himself there.

To return to my young colleague's theory, it is true that God will never ride roughshod over personality, or even over our social customs, provided they are not in conflict with his kingdom and his righteousness. But his kingdom will never bow to any culture. On the contrary, all nations, kingdoms and cultures are destined to submit to the kingdom of God (Romans 14:11). And the church, the sharp cutting-edge of that kingdom, must not be tailored to people's cultural or personal preferences.

Your small corner or God's great expanse?

The church issue must be faced. It's no use sitting alone, each of us in his own small corner. Since we are all 'living stones' being built together into a spiritual house, we are an integral part of each other (1 Peter 2:5). Neither can any one local church manage on its own, aloof from the rest of the body of Christ. We must agree to build together *in alignment with the Word of God.*

God is not multi-optional. Jesus said, 'I am the way' (John 14:6). He depicted the path to life as 'narrow' and the access to it through a 'small' gate. The road which is broad and accommodating, with room for all the diverse and contradictory views of opinionated religion, is invariably the path to destruction (Matthew 7:13-14).

On Mount Carmel Elijah confronted a nation who had abandoned God with the challenge: 'How long will you waver between two opinions?' (1 Kings 18:21). He didn't present them with a catalogue of alternatives or a list of 'take your pick' choices. There were only two options: right or wrong, light or dark, God or idols – life or death.

The nation had been called to make a similar choice in the early days of its history. Poised to cross into the promised land after forty years of wandering through the wilderness, God's word had come to them through his servant Moses. It was an historic word which remains relevant to every generation: 'I have set before you life and death, blessings and curses' (Deuteronomy 30:19).

This, then, is God's bottom line. He does not confuse us with multiple choices but presents us with two clearly defined options on which to make our decision. There are no complexities to wrestle with. There is no need to fast and pray or seek the combined wisdom of many counsellors, because the choice is clear – life or death.

And just in case there remains any lingering doubt, the Lord adds a far from gentle nudge in the right direction, saying, *'Choose life'* (Deuteronomy 30:19).

7

God is still looking

It just wasn't fair. Here she was, running herself off her feet, busy with all the preparations, while her sister just sat there, oblivious to all that needed doing.

'Can't Mary see that I need help?' she thought crossly. And unable to contain herself any longer, her irritation spilled over on to Jesus, who really should have noticed how unfair the situation was!

'Don't you care that my sister has left me to do the work by myself?' she challenged him. 'Tell her to help me!'

But the gentle rebuke of Jesus revealed a priority of a different kind: 'Martha. . . you are worried and upset about many things,' he replied, 'but only *one thing* is needed' (Luke 10:38-42).

And it was Mary who had recognised it.

Martha had allowed herself to be weighed down with all the activities of her serving. But Mary had 'chosen what is better' and, sitting at the feet of Jesus, far from wasting time, she listened carefully to every word he said.

Jesus was presenting Martha with a clear option: 'Your work or my word'.

One thing at a time

As we saw in the last chapter, there is only one way for us to go – God isn't multi-optional. The church loyalty question is basically simple. But so often the decisions which confront us seem complex and confusing. Where do we start?

In his grace God makes it easy for us. Asking us to deal with only *one thing* at a time, he faces us with a priority choice which helps to set the pattern for resolving every remaining issue.

Martha had to learn that, although the practical things of life have to be done, time must be taken just to sit at Jesus' feet and soak up his word. Knowing her weakness in this area, God placed her in a situation where that specific weakness would be revealed and a decision be required: her work or God's word.

To take another example, see how the Lord dealt with a young man who came to him seeking eternal life. He was a religious young man, moral, upright, honourable, likeable, regular at synagogue, obedient to the law – and rich.

The particular stumbling-block in his life was an attitude that allowed the temporary security of his wealth to rob him of the real security of peace with God and treasure in heaven. And Jesus highlighted this basic issue.

'One thing you lack,' he said – and once again the simple options came into focus as Jesus effectively offered him a choice: 'Your money or my life' (Mark 10:17-22).

It wasn't wrong for the young man to be rich. It wasn't wrong for him to have possessions. But Jesus was requiring a greater priority in the man's life than his possessions – to the extent that he would be willing to part with it all.

In effect Jesus was saying, 'What is your priority? What comes first in your thinking when you make decisions? What is the most important thing to you?'

If it isn't him – if it isn't the Lord Jesus Christ, and doing his will – then God will take you one step at a time, facing you with one issue at a time, until he becomes your priority and everything else finds its true perspective in relation to him.

A man after God's own heart

God described King David as a man after his own heart (Acts 13:22). It isn't surprising, then, to discover that he was a man of straightforward decisions.

'*One thing* I ask of the Lord,' said David (Psalm 27:4). His request was for a life of fellowship with God. To be overawed, not with the splendour of the Lord's house, but by the beauty of the Lord himself. Not to depart from the house of the Lord in confusion, but in confidence, knowing that he had sought the Lord and found him. He saw his choice as one between ritual and reality, liturgy and life, and he was choosing life.

Paul, likewise, had a singleness of purpose. '*One thing* I do,' he testified, 'I press on towards the goal' (Philippians 3:13-14).

There was a time when he had boasted of his traditions, holding and practising them more zealously than any of his contemporaries. But Jesus had broken into his life and taken hold of him. All he could do now was press on to attain the goal for which the Lord had laid hold of him.

The choice for him – as for many church members today – was go on or go back; the past or the future; history or destiny. And Paul had no difficulty choosing: he was going on.

But what about us? What are our priorities? How are we choosing? Are we gravitating to a place where we find comfort and confidence in our own ability and respectability? Or are we reaching for the one thing we lack, and responding to the call for radical discipleship, with all its implications for local church loyalty?

If we look back at the biblical characters we have just considered we will find that our own priorities and allegiance are based on very similar criteria to theirs.

Are we, like Martha, attracted to a full social programme, a hive of activity and a chance to shine? Or are we motivated, like Mary, towards the one really needful thing – a clear revelation of the word of God?

Do we tend towards ritual and regulation? Or, like David, is the one thing we desire not ceremony but a living relationship with the Lord? Are we dyed-in-the-wool traditionalists or, like Paul since his dynamic encounter with Jesus, are we doing the one thing God has called us to do – pressing on to the fulfilment of our destiny?

What is God looking for? Paul explained that the 'one thing' that gave purpose to his life was the outworking of a divine intervention in it. He knew that he had been 'taken hold of'. He was conscious of having been chosen by God, sought by him, and found and enrolled into his service (Philippians 3:12-14).

God is continually seeking men and women who will respond to him in just such a way. Ever since the fall of Adam, when God sought him in the garden, he has been looking for those with whom he can renew fellowship. And when the right time came he sent forth his Son, who described his own commission like this: 'The Son of Man came to seek and to save what was lost' (Luke 19:10).

But our salvation is far greater than 'sins forgiven and a home in heaven'. The Lord sought and saved us not just to wait longingly for the 'sweet by and by' but to make a dynamic impact on the 'nasty here and now'!

Paul's prayer for the church was, 'That the eyes of your heart may be enlightened in order that you may know the hope to which he has called you' (Ephesians 1:18). That is, that we should understand the call of God upon our lives and so be motivated to do the works he has called us to do.

You see, to fulfil the call of God, something more than a mere intellectual appreciation of his will for us is required. We must grasp in our hearts that God has called each of us, individually, to achieve great things for him.

You may say, 'Well, I'm nobody special. What strength or ability do I have to do anything for God?' And we can easily convince ourselves that we have nothing to offer him and are totally unusable. But, strange though it may seem, this is the very qualification we need!

As Paul wrote to the Corinthians: 'Brothers, think of what you were when you were called. Not many of you were wise by human standards; not many were influential; not many were of noble birth. But God chose the foolish things of the world to shame the wise; God chose the weak things of the world to shame the strong. He chose the lowly things of the world and the despised things - and the things that are not - to nullify the things that are, so that no-one may boast before him' (1 Corinthians 1:26-29).

God takes us, and by the power of his Holy Spirit makes us into something we could never be in our own strength. What we are not, he makes us to be - channels of his life and power, chosen and called to impact and change the world.

Our success for God is already guaranteed by the very fact that he has chosen us, for God never does anything frivolously. He knew when he chose you what he wanted you to do and be. And when you really understand the greatness of God's call upon your life, you will be thrilled with a sense of your destiny and motivated into his purposes.

But, again, it requires a right response from you. Ask God to show you his purpose for *your* life. Pray Paul's prayer in Ephesians 1 for yourself and allow God to impress upon you an understanding of his call upon your life. Not you as one more out of millions, but you as an individual, cherished by God and chosen by him before birth for a destiny which only you can fulfil.

'I looked for a man among them'

Before we leave this chapter let's look quickly at some examples of the Lord's search through humanity to find people who will respond to him.

Conversing with a woman at the well of Sychar, Jesus gave her a precious insight into the kind of people God is seeking. 'A time is coming and has now come,' he said, 'when the true worshippers will worship the Father in spirit and truth, for they are the kind of worshippers the Father seeks' (John 4:23).

God is looking for a people who will *worship* him with all their hearts – that is one of the hallmarks of the true people of God. Paul, contrasting the born again believers with those still bound in dead, legalistic tradition, and referring to the old practice of circumcision, said, 'We are the true circumcision, who worship in the Spirit of God and glory in Christ Jesus and put no confidence in the flesh' (Philippians 3:3 NASB).

Restored relationship with God will always express itself in extravagant praise and worship. The psalmist tells us that God is enthroned upon, or inhabits, the praises of his people (Psalm 22:3 margin). And he continues to look for such a people among whom he can feel at home.

King David really knew how to praise and worship the Lord! His psalms are full of stirring calls to join him in glorifying the God of his salvation, and Jerusalem must have resounded with the sound of music and singing during his golden reign. He even invented musical instruments in his desire to expand the expressions of his creative worship.

Samuel the prophet described God's choice of David like this: 'The Lord has sought out a man after his own heart' (1 Samuel 13:14). And the Lord's own assessment of David was: 'I have found David son of Jesse a man after my own heart; *he will do everything I want him to do'* (Acts 13:22).

The Lord continues to look for those, like David, whose hearts will respond to his own, and who are willing, from the heart, to do all he asks of them – a people willing to serve his purposes here and now (Acts 13:36).

Tragically, soon after the glorious age of David's reign, the nation slipped into a decline which culminated in a humiliating defeat and captivity in Babylon. But even here God raised up his prophets to bring his word to his exiled people.

Ezekiel revealed the heart of God to this rebellious nation, portraying the Lord searching among the teeming masses of Jerusalem for just one person who would, by his righteous intercession, turn the tide of disaster from the beleaguered city.

'I looked for a man among them who would build up the wall and stand before me in the gap on behalf of the land so that I would not have to destroy it, but I found none' (Ezekiel 22:30).

What an indictment! Among all the religious multitudes there wasn't one person to take the side of the Lord. Not one voice raised in God's cause. Not one arm stretched out to rebuild the devastated city. Not one foot to stand steadfastly in the gap.

Tragic, yes, but the greater tragedy is when, having failed to learn its lesson, we repeat the past in the present. The Babylonian captivity may be over, but many have allowed the pressures of life to ensnare them and pull them away from God, carrying them away like captives to a strange land. Gone is the joy of their salvation, and gone is the exciting tug of destiny on their lives.

Others cower behind the cracking walls of a beseiged church, hoping only to survive until Jesus comes, whereas in God's plan the church was built to be invading and invincible. He is looking for men and women who will rise up out of the dust of defeatism and fatalistic acceptance of the way things are.

He is looking for a people who will rebuild the ruins of many generations, who will take their stand in the purpose of God, and who will believe to see the restoration of Zion – a church restored and on the move.

8

Church-splitting

Sooner or later, someone is going to object that what I have been saying will inevitably lead to church-splitting and sheep-stealing. But let me state quite categorically: *that is not the aim of this book.*

My one sincere desire is that all the people of God move into all the purposes of God. But I am well aware that, while some are eager to move on, others are firmly entrenched and refuse to budge – and as the old song says, when an irresistible force meets an immovable object, something's got to give!

Accusations of church-splitting and sheep-stealing will inevitably arise. So I intend to deal fairly with these issues over the next two chapters in order to put your minds at rest.

Locked into the past

Throughout history, every move of God has shown that it cannot be contained within the religious environment from which it emerged. That environment somehow seems to blind people to the next revelation of God's truth and life.

Many Jews, anxiously awaiting the coming of the Messiah,

completely missed it when he did come. Refusing to accept Jesus as the promised Saviour of the world, and closing their eyes and ears to all he did and said, they remained locked into the law of the Old Testament. Being bound to the past, they completely missed the blessing of what God was doing in the present.

They never knew what it was to experience the reality of God as a close, loving Father, or the forgiveness of their sin through Christ's blood. Nor were they able to experience the power of the Holy Spirit within them, raising them up into resurrection life – that abundant life which Jesus lived on earth and longs for each one of us to experience too.

New wine needs new wineskins

How could such a tragedy for so many people have occurred? Jesus described it like this: 'No-one pours new wine into old wineskins. If he does, the new wine will burst the skins, the wine will run out and the wineskins will be ruined. No, new wine must be poured into new wineskins' (Luke 5:37-38).

There is no place for rigidity or inflexibility in the kingdom of God. Our first allegiance must be to *life,* not to structure. It must be to the new wine of God's ongoing purposes, not the old skin of yesterday's blessing.

If a structure is unchangeable and inflexible it must be abandoned, because where desperate attempts are made to contain the new wine (move of God) within the rigidity of a tradition or denomination, split wineskins (churches) are inevitable.

For example, let me describe a hypothetical situation. A local congregation is exposed to biblical teaching foreign to its traditions. It could be baptism in water, baptism in the Holy Spirit, divine healing, spiritual gifts or any number of other scriptural truths not previously practised in that church.

A section of the membership is gripped by this 'new truth', and is convinced by the Holy Spirit that it must be embraced and obeyed. Like the merchant in the parable who finds the pearl of great price (Matthew 13:45-46), they are motivated by the joy of possessing more of the revelation of God.

Within the same congregation, however, are the hard core traditionalists. They will not tolerate these deviations from established practice, and are quick to point out that the doctrinal position of their denomination effectively forbids them. Those who have determined to obey the Word of God are no longer welcome, being viewed as heretics or, at best, troublemakers. And, in all honesty, these no longer feel at home among many of the people to whom they were once joined.

A division has taken place, and invariably it is those who have embraced the new who leave the old. Those who are left may find some perverse comfort in misapplying such scriptures as, 'They went out from us, but they did not really belong to us' (1 John 2:19). And, inevitably, they accuse the leavers of splitting the church.

The question is: Who *really* split the church? Was it not those who refused to move with God?

Do you recall David and Jean, back in chapter two, and their experience? Once with a two-hundred-strong congregation, their church had clearly known the blessing of God in the past. But many steadfastly refused to allow God to operate among them in any way with which they weren't one hundred per cent familiar. And they refused to listen to the warnings given by visiting ministers.

Eventually the church split into factions – those trying desperately to introduce the new, and those trying equally desperately to keep it out. Finally, many were forced to leave and find elsewhere the freedom into which God was longing to bring all of his people.

In David and Jean's own words: 'We were dying on our feet, but the environment made change impossible.'

Don't get left behind

As God moves, we must move with him – or be left behind.

As God reveals more of himself to us we must be prepared to make the changes that revelation requires. We dare not, like Israel of old and many in David and Jean's church, remain locked into the past, refusing to accommodate change.

This necessity for the church to remain open to God's continual unveiling of himself – sometimes known as 'progressive revelation' – isn't a new one. Jesus himself explained to his disciples: 'I have much more to say to you, more than you can now bear. But when he, the Spirit of truth, comes, he will guide you into all truth. He will not speak on his own; he will speak only what he hears, and he will tell you what is yet to come. He will bring glory to me by taking from what is mine and making it known to you' (John 16:12-14).

The same idea is powerfully expressed in the charge which John Robinson, pastor to the Pilgrim Fathers, gave to his flock as they prepared to return to England from Holland and then go on to America:

> 'I charge you before God and his blessed angels, that you follow me no further than you have seen me follow the Lord Jesus Christ. If God reveals anything to you by any other instrument of his, be as ready to receive it as you were to receive any truth by my ministry for I am verily persuaded the Lord hath more truth yet to break forth out of his holy Word.
>
> 'For my part I cannot sufficiently bewail the condition of those reformed churches which are come to a period [full stop] in religion, and will go, at present, no further than the instrument of their reformation.
>
> 'The Lutherans cannot be drawn to go beyond what Luther saw: whatever part of his will our God has revealed to Calvin, they will rather die than embrace it; and the Calvinists, you see, stick fast where they were left by that

> great man of God, who yet saw not all things.
>
> 'This is a misery much to be lamented, for though they were burning and shining lights in their times, yet they penetrated not into the whole counsel of God; but were they now living, would be as willing to embrace further light as that which they first received, for it is not possible the Christian world should come so lately out of such thick anti-Christian darkness and that perfection of knowledge should break forth at once.'[1]

Before somebody points out to me the warning contained in Revelation 22:18 let me quickly add that not for a moment am I suggesting that we should expect to receive any fresh revelation that is extra-biblical. Only what is in the Word of God can be in the will of God.

But I stand with John Robinson, being fully persuaded that the Lord has much truth still to break forth out of his holy Word. And like the psalmist I pray, 'Open my eyes that I may see wonderful things in your law' (Psalms 119:18).

The apostle Paul lived at a time when the gospel, the mystery of God which had been kept secret for long ages past, was being supernaturally revealed through Jesus and being seen to be confirmed in every respect by the writings of the prophets (Romans 16:25-27). It was imparted by divine revelation but endorsed by biblical confirmation.

In other words, when God revealed himself through Jesus he did nothing he hadn't already promised to do in his Word. It was simply that what had been closed to people's understanding before had now been opened.

And along with these early pioneers, the psalmist, Paul and John Robinson, we too must be ready and willing to receive a greater revelation of God and move into the next phase of his recovery programme for us.

The word 'pilgrim' isn't just a quaint description of those early religious historic adventurers. It is an apt word to apply to all the children of God, those who, like the heroes of faith in past generations, confess they are strangers and exiles on the earth, seeking a heavenly country (Hebrews 11:13-16).

We are not called to be settlers but pioneers, constantly pushing back the frontiers of our experience with God. The overriding pull of God's ultimate – that city designed and built by him – should be dictating our conduct in the immediate. For what we see determines how we live. If we are looking for the city of God, we won't have the time or the desire to build anything less. And if our vision is clear we will get on with its building whatever the cost.

'Come in' and 'come on'

Divisions and factions are not all bad news. Paul strongly rebuked the Corinthian church for forming 'personality cults' and fomenting party spirit, but he did point out the positive nature of divisions: 'Doubtless there have to be factions or parties among you in order that they who are genuine and of approved fitness may become evident and plainly recognised among you' (1 Corinthians 11:19 Amplified Bible).

The wheat must be separated from the chaff. The precious must be extracted from the worthless (see Jeremiah 15:19 NASB). The pure must be extracted from the impure. True spirituality must be separated from empty tradition.

But separation isn't an end in itself. God only moves with a purpose. What is approved must be separated from what is not approved *in order that the approved may be clearly seen.* Separation alone is pointless – it must be separation to the Lord and to his purposes. Just as he called Abram out of Ur, and Israel out of Egypt, his call to 'come out' is always a call to 'come in' and 'come on'.

Ask yourself again the question: Who really splits the church? And as you consider the answer, remember that God's purpose is greater than just 'you' or 'me'. There is a world to heal, people to save, and God has already chosen how he is going to achieve it.

Will we – and our church connections – be a help to him, or a hindrance?

Chapter 8 NOTES

1 Quoted in *The Pilgrim Church,* by E.H. Broadbent (Marshall Pickering)

9

Sheep-stealing

The literal crime of sheep-stealing has always been a serious offence. In days gone by you could be hung or deported for it.

I have the sneaky feeling that quite a few would welcome the reintroduction of such punishment today – for those they consider guilty of its religious counterpart!

So-called sheep-stealing within the church has always been an emotive issue. Seen as a direct attack upon a man's ability to lead a church, it threatens his sense of personal adequacy and can lead to all manner of upsets, disputes and broken relationships, not to mention the hurt and bitterness which try, sometimes successfully, to get a lasting foothold within him.

But to get to the root of the issue we must look at it from a biblical perspective and find out, first, what sheep-stealing is and, second, what it isn't.

Finding the real stumbling-block

To begin with, the Bible portrays the church as *God's* flock, purchased with his own blood (Acts 20:28), so the sheep cannot be stolen from a pastor, or any other church leader. He doesn't own them. He guards and guides them, shepherds and pastures them, but God alone possesses them. So if one of God's sheep is actually 'stolen', it can only be stolen from God, by an enemy of God who comes with only one goal in mind: 'to steal and kill and destroy' (John 10:10).

Imagine that I'm the pastor of a large, flourishing church in a town where there are many churches moving on with God, as well as all kinds of devil-inspired activities such as spiritualist churches, fortune-telling and other occult practices (see Deuteronomy 18:10-12).

If a sheep should be stolen – that is, fails to embrace genuine biblical teaching and is lured away by the deceitfulness of Satan – then I must do what good shepherds have always done: I must lay down my life for the sheep.

Instead of wallowing in self-pity, or raging with vindictive recriminations, I must go out and seek it until I find it. Confronting the lion, attacking the bear or chasing off the wolf, I must rescue the sheep and bring it home safe and sound. That is my responsibility as a man called by God to shepherd his sheep.

If, however, the flock begins to leave me spontaneously, I need to review my own shepherding skill – for my own sake, as well as for the sake of the remaining church members.

I must look at the situation honestly, asking myself and God: Why have they left, and to what have they moved on? Have they seen some truth I haven't seen? Could it be that they have experienced something fresh of God that, until now, I have been too afraid, too proud or too sceptical to accept myself?

Have I been a good shepherd? Have I strengthened the sickly and healed the diseased? Have I bound up the brokenhearted and brought back the scattered? (See Ezekiel 34:1-6.) Have I fed them in the rich pastures of God's Word? Have I led them in the paths of righteousness, or indeed along any path at all? If I myself have nowhere to go – no path to tread, no destination to reach – how can the flock follow me? (See Matthew 15:14.)

Have I really fulfilled my leadership responsibilities to the sheep, or have I become a stumbling-block to them?

What will be your epitaph?

If you are in leadership then you must ask these questions about yourself. If you aren't in leadership then you must ask yourself the questions about those who are. They may be hard to ask, and even harder to answer, but they must be faced if we are to see the situation and ourselves realistically.

To be a leader one must lead. To be a godly leader one must lead in the ways of God. And we must face the fact that many churches receiving people from other congregations today are not stealing sheep but rescuing them. They grow better grass and provide greater security. They allow God to move unrestricted in their church, and they give a stronger lead. So, naturally, they attract those who desire to be fulfilled in their walk with God and who want to respond to his call upon their lives.

There are many fellowships of God's people now emerging who can confidently say, like Moses, 'Come with us and we will do you good' (Numbers 10:29 NASB). But today is no different from history. Such moves still involve, among other elements, harsh dispute and jealousy.

Jesus himself faced that very problem. In his ministry to the 'lost sheep of Israel' and in commissioning his disciples into the same ministry (Matthew 15:24; 10:6), he was taking a deliberately provocative step. Though his motive was compassion for the people, whom he saw as 'harassed and helpless, like sheep without a shepherd' (Matthew 9:36), he knew that the Pharisees' only concern would be his growing popularity, which would pose a threat to their own status and influence with the people.

In their eyes, with his constant call to 'come to me', he was setting himself up in competition with the religious establishment and stealing sheep which were rightfully theirs.

But they themselves cared little for the sheep. And however much righteous indignation they projected, however strong their presentation of themselves as guardians of the truth, even the fearful and indecisive Pilate was well aware that the Pharisees had handed Jesus over to death through nothing more than unholy envy (Mark 15:9-10).

It is easy to criticise but how would *we* respond – whether in a leadership role or not – in a similar situation?

Would we be prepared to listen to those leaving us and really seek God for what he wanted, keeping ourselves open to the possibility that those leaving might actually be right – or at least partly right? Or would we shut ourselves away from the opportunity of any fresh revelation from God, determined to 'stick to our guns' whatever?

The minister in Alan and Gillian's church refused point-blank to recognise the baptism and gifts of the Holy Spirit. When Alan and Gillian eventually got baptised in the Spirit, his response was a mixture of bewilderment and resentment. He accused them of not accepting his shepherding authority, and at no time did he display any willingness to reconsider the issue, even though his wife was a beautiful, Spirit-filled woman herself.

'He dismissed the difference in his wife simply by saying that she had a different personality from him,' Gillian explained. 'He certainly didn't accept that she had anything he himself didn't have.

'We left, as did about a dozen other people over the space of a couple of years – all of us looking for spiritual links which would enable us to fulfil our walk with God. He continued as minister for a further two years until he had a nervous breakdown, and now he spends his whole time studying. His wife, though she still goes to church, works full-time to support the family and seems to have no spark of life left in her. It's a really tragic situation.

'If only he had been willing to listen to us, things could have been so different, but fear and pride got in the way and he couldn't accept what God was doing.'

He couldn't accept what God was doing! What a sad epitaph. But to how many people does it apply? Could it apply to your minister, or even to you?

Fran and Gordon had a similar experience, but one showing more promise of change. The minister in their church didn't believe in baptism in water, and maintained that baptism in the Holy Spirit was something that happened automatically once you made a decision to go to church. Having experienced both baptisms, Fran and Gordon tried to explain the scriptural position to the minister. But he was unwilling to listen.

'He was very angry, and somewhat resentful, when we got baptised in water, and he wouldn't accept what we had to say about the Holy Spirit,' Fran remembered.

'He didn't want us to leave, though, so for a while we stayed on and tried to bring into the church something of what we had found. We suggested that the church meet together before the Sunday evening meeting to pray about what God really wanted for his church. Some people seemed quite interested, but the minister really wasn't keen on it and after three or four weeks it stopped.

'There was nothing more we could do, so we left. But then there was a sudden change of attitude on the minister's part. He used to spend a few hours in prayer one morning a week, and he began ringing me up, telling me what he was going to be praying for and asking me to support him in it. Recently he told us that he was looking with interest at the way our new church is growing.

'He has now retired but has said that should anyone ask him which church to go to, he would direct them to ours. I still don't think he accepts baptism in the Holy Spirit or in water as the Bible speaks of it, but he has certainly mellowed.'

Doctrinal positions and attitudes can take a long time to change. And it has to be admitted that the situation hasn't been helped by the often insensitive and dogmatic attitudes of some who have 'seen the light'. But if we remain open for God to change us and are willing to accept that we might need adjustment on some issues, he will gradually turn us around until we are facing in the right direction.

Seeing ourselves as stewards

In sharp contrast to the Pharisees, John the Baptist is the greatest example I know of a man able to let go of his sheep so that they could move on further into God's purposes.

What do you think he felt as he began to lose his disciples? There he was, describing Jesus as 'the Lamb of God', when two of his own men, hearing this, left him and went after Jesus. What's more, the Lord was actually welcoming them! When they asked where he was staying, far from rebuking them and sending them back to John in repentance, he invited them to come and see (John 1:35-39).

The Pharisees soon learned that Jesus was making and baptising more disciples than John and, in keeping with their character, no doubt sought to exploit the situation to their own advantage. When our adversaries begin to gloat as the other man's work starts to outgrow our own, it's not too difficult to cope because we are well aware of their motives.

It is much more difficult to keep in perspective the concerned reports of those who through friendship and loyalty have stayed with us. John's remaining disciples were quick to point out to him the Lord's growing success, and to tell him how the multitudes who had once flocked to John were now flocking to Jesus (John 4:1; 3:27-28).

A man less secure in God than John would immediately feel threatened, and no doubt find himself relentlessly pressured by a competitive spirit. But John wasn't in competition with Jesus. He saw himself not as the owner of those whom God had placed in his care, but merely as God's steward – one who was diligently looking after God's property.

As a servant of God doing the work of God, he had prepared the way of the Lord, and his ministry was now fulfilled. And he himself was fulfilled in the knowledge that, from now on, he must decrease while Jesus increased (see John 3:30). His followers had not been stolen, they had simply been divinely transferred into the continuing plan of God.

In a message to the congregation of the Pisidian Antioch synagogue recorded in Acts 13, Paul made some interesting observations concerning certain characters from Israel's history. Speaking fleetingly of King Saul, he summed up his whole reign with the words, 'After [God] had removed him . . .' (Acts 13:22 NASB). Remember, by the way, that Saul was rejected long before he was actually removed; continued existence does not prove divine acceptance (1 Samuel 13:13-14).

But speaking of John the Baptist, Paul records that he was 'completing his work' (Acts 13:25). That is, he was seeing through to a conclusion the work God had entrusted to him. He wasn't attempting to perpetuate into a movement what the Lord had sent only to impact the moment.

His is the example for us to follow. But down through history, the sad evidence is that what God has imparted as a revelation for the church as a whole, people have accommodated as a denomination for the few.[1] As a result, many who were once on the cutting edge of God's prophetic word are now more concerned with maintaining the identity of their past than trying to live out what God is doing in the present.

Like the minister in Alan and Gillian's church, having placed their security in their achievements rather than in God, they hold on to the past, fearful of losing what they falsely think they have. Instead they could (like Bob, the former church deacon we met in the first chapter) be reaching into God for bigger and better things and moving on in the forefront of his purposes again.

The people of God must continually be encouraged away from what is rejected and redundant, into what is relevant and revelatory concerning God's purposes *now*. There is, of course, a sense in which God's purpose remains unchanged, but he is for ever moving forward in the outworking of that purpose, and we must be flexible enough to move with him.

So, if the sheep are disappearing from your church, whether it be the odd few, or in droves, ask yourself why. And determine, with God's help, to answer with complete honesty. It may have nothing to do with the way your church is run or how the flock is pastored. But then again, it might.

Suddenly to realise that one's life and ministry, at least during the last few years, have been spent promoting the rejected and the redundant can be shattering, to say the least, and hard to come to terms with. So, also, are the feelings of failure and condemnation which naturally follow. But God is bigger than all our failings put together – he shed his blood for them all. As we release it all to him he will show us the way through and set our feet back on the right track.

Then we can be found once again in the full flow of the purpose of God and say, as could King David (Acts 13:36), that we have served God's purpose in our generation.

Chapter 9 NOTES

1 For a detailed look at this principle in church history see *Church Adrift,* by David Matthew (Harvestime)

10

Red herrings

Certain objections are regularly raised by those who have been challenged to move on with God.

For various reasons they feel unable (or is it unwilling?) to change, and some of the arguments used have become so common that they have passed into a kind of religious folklore. They seem to have taken on the authority, if not of Scripture itself, then at least of a kind of widely accepted 'apocrypha'.

I would like to reel in a few of those red herrings – and (in the next chapter) roast some of those old chestnuts. It's high time that religious myths masquerading as spiritual reasons were well and truly exploded.

'The church will always be a mixture'

A favourite compromising attitude takes comfort from the idea that the church is doomed to mixture until Jesus comes back. And therefore whatever stand you make for God, wherever you go, there will always be a mixture of those who want to go on with God and those who don't.

The idea seems to have come from a basic misunderstanding

of Jesus' parable of the weeds in Matthew 13.

Jesus described the kingdom of heaven as being like a man who sowed good seed in his field, but while he slept, along came the enemy and sowed weeds among the wheat. On discovering this, the man's servants wanted to go and pull the weeds out immediately. But he stopped them, explaining that both must grow together until the harvest, when the weeds would be collected and burned.

Many have understood this to mean that we have no alternative but to suffer mixture until Jesus comes back for his church. But that's not what Jesus said. Explaining the parable to his disciples, he told them: 'The good seed stands for the sons of the kingdom. The weeds are the sons of the evil one' and 'the field is the world' (Matthew 13:37-38).

The field is the *world!* Righteousness and unrighteousness are to be found together in one field – the world, not the church.

The world is inhabited by believers and unbelievers alike, and will be until Jesus returns, but there is no place for mixture in the church. The church is to be peopled only by the redeemed – those who have repented, believed the gospel and been born again by the Spirit of God.

You may recall Kenneth, whom we met back in chapter five. His desire to be true to the Word of God resulted in his leaving a church where many just couldn't see the necessity for it. The majority on the church council were unbelievers and, not surprisingly, these were the ones most anxious to see him leave.

If a person hasn't been born again by the Spirit of God he simply can't understand the things of the Spirit (1 Corinthians 2:14), so how can you expect to build with him in God's way? It just won't work.

A less radical mixture, but still one that needs avoiding, is the mixing of those envisioned by God with those who hamper his work by refusing to allow the Holy Spirit to guide the church – insisting on retaining their man-made traditions instead.

Mike was one of a number of elders in a church in north-west England. Evidence of mixture was already apparent in resistance to the Holy Spirit and various biblical practices. But the issue which finally exposed people's attitudes was the elders' proposal to abolish the constitution. The elders were of one mind about this and had given several weeks' notice to allow plenty of opportunity for the presentation and debate of the issues.

'During this period it became clear where loyalties lay – and a split became inevitable,' Mike recalled. 'Rather than push the issue to a formal meeting, thus forcing a split, we elders recognised that, since it was no longer possible for us to function in the light of our convictions either within that congregation or within the denominational framework, we would lay down our eldership. This we announced at the next church meeting, indicating our individual decisions to withdraw from membership.

'The reaction to our leaving was mixed. For some, it meant a welcome return to more traditional ways. Others felt a genuine sense of loss and grief. While for still others it meant a decision to leave also.

'Obviously, it was a very difficult time for me, but I have never doubted that I did the right thing,' Mike affirmed. 'We must recognise that mixture and unbelief are the enemies of faith and the fulfilled walk. Either they go, or you must.'

Mike was under no illusions about the issues at stake. It was a case of being either for the Lord or against him. With the Lord or without him. The two couldn't be combined. And as he took that step of faith, God brought him into a whole new spiritual dimension.

'I now belong to a church where I have experienced great spiritual growth – in my faith; my personal vision; my understanding of God's Word and living in the truth of it; and the whole area of order in my personal and family life. One of the main things, though, is that I have been challenged by the reality and integrity of people living by the Scriptures.'

There is no place for mixture in the church. And just in case a lingering doubt still remains, the Lord makes the position clear in Paul's letter to the Corinthian church: 'Come out from them and be separate.'

Note this, however: *We should not in any way look down on those who haven't seen what we have seen. Neither does the Lord love them any less than he loves us.* It's simply that the Lord is calling us to commit ourselves wholeheartedly to working and walking in his ways. As we have seen over and over again, it inevitably involves cost. But there is no need to be afraid of that cost. As in Mike's case, God gives back to us far more than we can ever give up.

'But the church needs me'

Issuing from a misunderstanding of the nature of the church comes another familiar cry of despair: 'But if I leave, who will bear witness to the truth in this place?'

How many of God's people are held captive in unbelieving situations by a false sense of responsibility? How many are held back, feeling that the church needs them and that, if they leave, the church has even less chance of making it?

It's a genuine concern which many feel when they begin to weigh up the pros and cons of departing from a spiritually dead congregation. That concern is increased when – as is often the case – the one eager to serve well in the circumstances is often the organist, steward, youth leader, Sunday school teacher and missionary secretary, not to mention magazine editor, bookstall manager, flower rota arranger and general dogsbody!

He (or she) feels guilty just entertaining the thought of leaving, even though his enthusiasm has so far produced little, if any, response. Deadlines for evidence of change have come and gone, and still he seeks to convince himself that he is being faithful.

But faithful to what? Certainly not to the Word of God. Jesus himself gave clear instructions as to what our attitude should be towards any community refusing to respond to our sharing of the gospel: 'If any place will not welcome you *or listen to you,* shake the dust off your feet when you leave, as a testimony against them' (Mark 6:11).

Matthew records the same injunction, and Luke has it twice! History shows us that the apostles took it quite literally: when their message was rejected by the religious establishment this was exactly what Paul and Barnabas did (Acts 13:50-51).

Are you in a similar situation? Then maybe it's time to shake the dust off your feet - just like Chris and Tanya had to.

Chris joined the church in his youth and, after marrying Tanya (the minister's daughter), settled down as a youth group leader and lay preacher. But after a while things became very unsatisfactory.

'My father-in-law retired,' he explained, 'and we had a new, more active, minister who promised much but realised little in the way of actual progress. We worked very hard to support him and to help others and ourselves to grow, but we felt more and more isolated as others just settled for routine.

'Much of my preaching was falling on deaf ears and I was being restricted increasingly in what I was allowed to say because of my longing to see God moving among us in a powerful way. We were beginning to dry up and, rather than be forced to compromise any more, we left.

'The situation we were in - always hoping and praying for a positive change - was a real trap for us. And it's a trap for anyone wanting to go on with God. Our spiritual health was suffering but we still tried to fool ourselves that everything would be all right. A false sense of loyalty, and of being "needed", only clouded the real issue of a dying church which only wanted the Holy Spirit on its own terms.'

Chris and Tanya will always be thankful to God that they had their eyes opened to the reality of the situation in time. Realising the trap they had fallen into, they were able to act before their spiritual health suffered any more damage. Firmly shaking the dust off their feet, they refused to be held back in their own walk with God by any false sense of being a lifeline to the church.

So don't be afraid to shake the dust off your feet. It's not a question of being unfaithful; it's a spiritual principle which Jesus commanded us to observe. All we have to do is be obedient to his Word – and we can leave the consequences to him.

'Faithfulness is more important than success'

Many Christians are terrified of proving 'unfaithful'. I have often heard it preached that faithfulness is more important than success and that the highest commendation from the Lord is 'Well done, good and faithful servant.'

I agree with that one hundred percent. But it has produced in some minds the idea that the person who tenaciously sticks at something (whatever that something may be) with no reaping for his sowing, no return for his investment and no reward for his labour, is somehow on a more spiritual plane than the person who gets results.

But that is to ignore what the Bible teaches. You see, there is a spiritual law in operation which dictates that faithfulness will carry its own success. In the very parable from which we take the Lord's commendation for faithfulness (the parable of the talents in Matthew 25), *the faithful servants are those who have been successful.*

So don't be duped into believing that staying put in a situation, even though it achieves nothing, is the real test of faithfulness. It isn't! If you are being faithful in the truly biblical sense, obedient to God instead of being ruled by your emotions, you will also be successful.

11

Old chestnuts

Having dealt with the hindering attitudes in our own mind, we then have to face the comments and accusations of others. These invariably confront us whenever we make a determined stand for God.

Assuming we have now realised that we need to leave the past behind and live for the future, let's consider three arguments often used against us, and how we should respond to them.

'Better the devil you know . . .'

If we decide to leave one local church in favour of another, some will try to trouble us with doubts about where we are going. At their fingertips they have a whole repertoire of hair-raising stories. After giving us the full gory details, they conclude: 'So don't you think you'd be safer staying where you are? After all, let's face it, better the devil you know than the devil you don't!'

'Better the devil you know'? That must be one of the most ridiculous sayings in the English language. There may be some kind of security in familiarity – even when the familiarity is an unpleasant one – but who wants to be acquainted with *any* kind of devil? Not us, I hope!

The fear of stepping out into the unfamiliar has never been, and never should be, an issue with any child of God determined to pursue his destiny.

Look at Abraham, that great forerunner of faith, who 'obeyed and went, even though he did not know where he was going' (Hebrews 11:8). Looking for the city of God, he had his heart set on God's best, wherever it might lead him, and we are called to walk in the footsteps of his faith (Romans 4:12).

Or imagine Peter desperately clinging to a storm-tossed boat. The wind is blasting and howling, the sea is pounding and he is frightened and confused. The sea has become one big, powerful enemy. But the boat, though unstable and vulnerable, is at least familiar. And he seeks a crumb of comfort in the well-known smells and feel of a vessel which is rapidly becoming more a threat of doom than a promise of deliverance.

Imagine, too, how his mounting fear in the face of the impending 'natural' disaster must have grown into full-blown terror at the sight of a supernatural manifestation. Seeing a figure walking on the water, he is convinced he has seen a ghost!

With his thinking distorted by blind panic, Peter fails to recognise Jesus, mistaking the King of kings and Lord of lords for an object of terror to be avoided at all costs. Such a mistake could have had dire consequences. But, happily, the reassuring voice of Jesus breaks through the fear. At his command, Peter steps out of the boat and begins to walk towards him across the water.

Safe in the hands of God

Have similar things happened in your own life? Have you, too, failed to recognise God, cringing away from him in fear, simply because you have never seen him move in that way before? Clinging desperately to the known and afraid to step out into the unknown, have you let God pass you by?

'But I was afraid to move,' you cry, 'in case I made a mistake.'

It's true that what often holds us back is fear of making a mistake and of looking a fool in front of others. And it's possible for all of us to make mistakes. But if we never step out, how will we know whether we were right or not? Success is founded on experience, and if we just sit tight and never make a move we won't have any experience on which to found it.

Even if we do make a mistake we have the ultimate safety net. God just loves it when we step out for him and is always there to catch us if we stumble. He is far bigger than any mistake we can make and more than able to hold our heads above water. Isn't that just what he did for Peter when, after his first triumphant steps upon the water, he took his eyes off Jesus and, allowing the natural appearance of the situation to instil fear into him again, began to sink?

Peter may have felt a bit of a fool when he got back to the boat, but really he had no reason to. Of all the disciples he was the only one prepared to reach out in faith towards Jesus, stepping out of the familiar into the unknown, his one desire being to reach the Lord's side.

Scott and Rosemary stepped out in a similar way.

'We had been members of the church for about three years,' Rosemary recalled. 'We were very active as youth leaders, and in charge of the evangelism. That sounds good, but it obscured the fact that we were stagnating in our faith. After a while, though, I became aware of our lack of spiritual growth. The deacons, who were responsible for all decision-making, were very able businessmen but not spiritually motivated, and the pastor was continually frustrated at being outvoted by them at meetings.

'So, after much prayer, we decided to leave and find a church where we could grow and where the Holy Spirit was the decider in the direction of the church. At the time of leaving we had absolutely no idea where we would go, but there was no point in staying just for the sake of it.

'Our number one responsibility is for our own spiritual growth. If we aren't making progress then we must move on for the sake of the kingdom of God, because whatever our current responsibilities, we cannot fulfil them properly if we aren't making the personal spiritual progress we should be.'

So Scott and Rosemary moved on, stepping out into the unknown and placing themselves entirely in the hands of God. And did he let them down? Of course not! He soon provided them with what they were looking for: a deeper personal relationship with him, a warm, loving church and the challenge of biblical teaching on all areas of Christian life.

So don't be afraid to step out. God will look after you!

You, too, can walk on water!

Leaving behind a dying church to start a new fellowship with five other people, Glenn wasn't afraid to step out into the unknown. On the contrary, he was excited by the challenge of moving out in faith. And that new church is now a loving family of some forty Christians – working, praying, sharing, caring and building together, with genuine commitment and love for each other.

His testimony is one of success. But he was only successful because his attitude was right. When most were afraid to lose the comforting familiarity of a sinking boat, when the majority were held back by a false sense of security, Glenn was willing to step out for God in any way he asked. His eyes were not on what he was going into, or what he was leaving behind– they were firmly fixed on Jesus. And this is his advice for us:

'Your loyalty is towards God, who is seeking to bring you up in the rich environment of his family on earth. It's not towards any other collection of people or traditions where the life, joy and vigour of Christ isn't expressed. It always seems safer to stay with the familiar, but don't be pressured by the prejudices of those who are clearly missing the blessing of God.

'Get out of the boat, start walking, keep your eyes on Jesus and you won't regret it.'

It's sound advice. Throughout life we all fall victim to material and spiritual pressures and uncertainties. But how we respond to them is up to us. We can cringe back into what is familiar – storm-tossed as it is – or we can respond in obedience and faith, stepping boldly out into the unknown.

Is Jesus calling you to come? Then step out, and you'll discover that you, too, can walk on water.

'Rats desert a sinking ship'

Staying with the nautical theme for a while, this is a very destructive accusation. Though completely irrational, it is persuasive because it touches us at our point of vulnerability, questioning our faithfulness and integrity.

'Ah,' comes the response at our decision to move on, 'rats leaving the sinking ship, eh?'

The idea, of course, is to provoke in us an image of heroic selflessness on the part of those remaining. In our mind's eye we see the stoic captain keeping his post on the bridge, the band playing patriotic tunes of self-sacrifice and the great liner slipping peacefully below the waves with solemn dignity.

And where am I? There I am – a rat racing for safety as far from the sinking vessel as I can get!

But why should such a scene make me feel guilty? Surely, all it proves is that the rats are smarter than the people! If the ship is sinking, take to the boats – when we get to heaven no martyr's crowns will be handed out for suicide.

One of the greatest tragedies of the Bible is that Jonathan died with Saul when he could have lived with David. Yes, King Saul was Jonathan's father, but he had been rejected from the purposes of God. David was to reign in his place. And David and Jonathan both knew God had joined them together for a particular purpose (1 Samuel 23:16-18).

Yet Jonathan stayed with his father and, being in the wrong place at the wrong time, died with him on the battlefield.

We could argue that Jonathan was only being faithful to his father, and what else could we expect? But *loyalty is only to be commended when it springs from the genuinely spiritual – not from the merely sentimental.* As we have already observed, faithfulness to God should bring us to a place of success, not a place of despair. It isn't our responsibility to 'carry the can' for the rest of the congregation, as Fran discovered.

Unable to stand the dryness any longer, she and her husband left their church after several unsuccessful attempts to bring the life of God into it.

Their efforts had brought only heartbreak as they witnessed the persistent refusal to respond to God. Eventually they came to see that it wasn't up to them to carry the responsibility for other people's attitudes; each needed to respond to God for himself. And leaving was the only option if they were to develop their own walk with God.

'Follow God's prompting,' Fran advised, 'and he will never leave you at a dry church. And what he can do for you, he is perfectly capable of doing for the others. It's not your job to look after them. You tend to think that you can't leave a sinking ship, but in the end you'll just sink with it.'

Jonathan owed loyalty first and foremost to the Lord, not to his father, Saul. But, unwilling to let go of the past, he was unable to move into the future. And when the ship finally sank he was still on board and sank with it, robbed of the abundant life God had wanted to give him.

It's a tragic story of a man with great potential. And it is also a grave warning for those of us with conflicting loyalties which have effectively barricaded our way ahead with God.

'You'll never find what you're looking for!'

Finally, we have the full-frontal, double-barrelled shotgun approach. The first blast is intended to shatter my illusions: 'You'll never find the perfect church.' And the next assassinates my character: 'And even if you did it would cease to be perfect the moment you joined.'

This attitude is based on two false suppositions. First, it assumes the church is doomed to imperfection. And second, it infers that God has given up on me. Both concepts I strongly reject. God hasn't given up on me – or you – and has no intention of doing so. Individually, and as a church, 'we shall be like him', the Bible tells us (1 John 3:2).

So why is it that the expectations of so many of God's people never break through the barrier of the disappointments and failures of the past?

Look back at the testimonies in this book. Clearly people's lives have changed dramatically as they have cast off the dead and dying for the vital life of Christ. But their testimonies aren't perfect. To question them all in detail would be to uncover some doubts and fears about the steps they were taking. Would they adapt to the new environment? Was it really the place God wanted them to be? How would they cope with the hostility and criticism from those left behind?

For Colin and Hazel, their welcome at first was not as friendly as they could have wished. They would have loved another couple to come alongside them as they battled to cope with the leaving behind of old friends and familiar surroundings, but at first it just didn't happen. Now, close relationships are developing but, as they discovered, getting to know people takes time.

For others, like Kenneth back in chapter five, there is the awful feeling of redundancy as, leaving behind positions of leadership and other responsibility, they find themselves with nothing to do. In some cases, as with Chris and Tanya, the new church is itself going through a difficult time, making the first few months especially rocky.

In other cases the problem is 'culture shock' after what has been left behind. Unused to the lively worship and the zeal for God, many feel at first like a fish out of water.

It's not surprising. There is bound to be a certain amount of insecurity and confusion during a time of such spiritual and emotional upheaval. There are new patterns to adapt to, old ideas to shed – and though things can sometimes be great from the word 'go', often it takes some working at.

So don't despair if you've made a change but so far things aren't working out quite as you had hoped. Persevere!

Andrew and Elspeth found the early days in their new church a strange mixture of excitement and panic. People were warm and friendly, but both felt very much on the outside. Eventually, Andrew began to break through his emotional barrier, though it took much longer for Elspeth to overcome her fear of the new surroundings. But gradually, as she put her trust in God, he brought her through, and this is now their triumphant testimony:

'We have "grown up" spiritually. We have become part of a family and we now know where we are going. What a change! Once we were losers but now we are winners.'

For all these people it was worth the initial difficulties. God is seeing them through – and he will see us through, too. But we must be prepared for some heartaches as well as great joy. And we must resist the temptation to give up every time something goes wrong.

Pressing on

The history of failure is not doomed to repeat itself for ever. If the Word of God urges us to 'press on to maturity' (Hebrews 6:1 NASB), then God himself is convinced we can make it!

If we don't go for perfection, what is the alternative? Blessed imperfection? Shall we proclaim a substandard, shop-soiled, slightly stained kind of Christianity? One that motivates into a zeal that is one notch above 'apathy' and raises our expectations to somewhere near the level of confusion?

Someone once said: 'If you aim at nothing, you will hit it every time!' So don't lower your sights to conform to the prevailing acceptance of mediocrity. Look up. Aim high. Press on to the upward and high call of God in Christ Jesus.

Just in case any of us should be tempted into smugness by comparing ourselves with others, let's remember that our 'perfection' isn't measured by the other man's 'imperfection'. We cannot judge our success by the other's failure. God's infallible standard is Jesus Christ himself, and he alone is the pattern to which we are called to conform, the example we are expected to follow.

After Jesus had risen from the dead, he appeared to his disciples one day on the shore of Lake Galilee. He asked Peter, 'Do you love me? . . . Tend my lambs.' And again, 'Do you love me? . . . Shepherd my sheep.' And a third time, 'Do you love me? . . . Tend my sheep.' He then emphasised his commission to Peter by restating his claim on Peter's life: *'Follow me!'*

Peter's responsibility of ministry was thus shown to be directly related to his relationship with the Lord. But at that moment Peter turned and saw his friend, John.

'Lord, and what about this man?' Peter questioned. But Jesus replied, *'What is that to you? You follow me!'* (John 21:15-23 NASB). You see, our response to the call of the Lord doesn't depend on what the other man does, but on what the Lord commands *us* to do.

Some will say, 'You can't go that way. Why, brother So-and-so doesn't agree with that at all.' Then we will be presented with an impressive list of notable Christians who are vocal in their opposition to the 'new thing' that is drawing us. Some of them are influential and respected leaders. They have blessed many, maybe even had an input into our own lives. What are we to do?

What about this man? What about that man? The polite rebuke of Jesus is still the same: 'What is that to you?' Or to put it into the vernacular: 'Mind your own business – you follow me.'

12

No compromise

It doesn't seem to matter how hard we try. Whatever we do, however good our intentions are, there is always someone ready to oppose us, just waiting for the right moment to pull down what we are working so hard to build up.

Jesus experienced this. He came only to do God's will, and he lived, died and rose again perfectly fulfilling that will. Not once did he display the slightest hint of compromise. But his single-mindedness and dedication were continually opposed – and deliberately misrepresented – by the religious leaders of the time.

When we find ourselves consumed with a similar zeal we can expect similar reactions. Rumour flies, slander spreads, gossip creeps, accusations are thrown – and it all seems to be targeted at us.

When it's from only one or two people it's not so hard to cope with, but when we get a whole group or a whole congregation against us, all trying to squeeze us into their mould, it can be very hard to stand.

But never mind; we're not alone. In fact we're in elevated company! For not only Jesus, but every man and woman down through history who carried a true revelation and word from God, was strongly opposed – even within the body of genuine believers.

Elijah was called the 'troubler of Israel' (1 Kings 18:17). The prophet Jeremiah was threatened with death if he persisted with his prophetic burden. The apostle Paul was accused of teaching things that were unlawful. And the early Christians were angrily opposed as those who had turned the world upside down.

In more recent history, Martin Luther, in the face of assembled ecclesiastical antagonism, made his simple confession: 'Here I stand. I can do no other.'

So it should come as no surprise to us when we face insult, accusation and even ostracism because of our beliefs.

That was what happened to Chris and Tanya whom we met earlier. After initial anger from their minister, they eventually left the church on good terms, only to find some time later, to their horror, that the rest of the congregation had been told to keep away from them.

'It was horrible,' they recalled. 'People went from being brothers and sisters to being outright enemies. If they saw us in the street they would cross the road rather than speak. A few came to see us, but there were many lies and rumours spread about us. We felt really hurt and empty.'

A heartbreaking time for Chris and Tanya – and unavoidable if they were to press on with God. But it wasn't without its compensations. For by their obedience not only were they themselves released to move into all that God had prepared for them, but two of their worst critics, Geoff and Mavis, also had their lives turned upside down! And having met with God in a radical way this couple are now part of Chris and Tanya's church and two of their closest friends.

God never leaves us empty. What the devil takes away, God restores. Out of heartbreak he brings blessing. Here we have four people no longer frustrated and empty but moving on in the forefront of God's purposes, committed to him and to each other.

Taking 'the sovereign stance'

How do we handle criticism and opposition when it occurs? How do we cope with the well-meant but misguided advice, the scaremongering and the persuasive pressure?

The Bible indicates a particular attitude that we must take in such circumstances, an attitude we see displayed in the life of King David.

Psalm 38 portrays him under intense pressure, both mental and spiritual. His friends and family have separated from him. His enemies are many and powerful. In it all he feels he is being opposed merely for following what is good. But he endures it by adopting what I call 'the sovereign stance'.

In the face of wrong advice, criticism, argument and even plot and threat against him, this is how he kept his feet on the right path: 'I, like a deaf man, do not hear; and I am like a dumb man who does not open his mouth. Yes, I am like a man who does not hear, and in whose mouth are no arguments. For I hope in thee, O Lord' (Psalm 38:13-15 NASB).

Closing his ears to every sound but the voice of God and closing his mouth to avoid fruitless argument, he placed his situation totally in the hands of the Lord.

As far as we can, we should do the same. We may not find it easy to shut out the many voices in the world, or find perfect quiet away from the verbal strife. But we can determine not to contribute to them.

True, we should be prepared to give a reason for our actions and answer legitimate questions. And we should be ready to share with any person genuinely concerned about us. But we are not required to field every accusation that flies at us. And we don't have to be drawn into long, pointless and often hostile discussions with people more interested in having an argument than seeking the truth.

We may not be able to stop everything from coming in, but we can certainly control what goes out!

We see this attitude very clearly in Jesus, who displayed 'the sovereign stance' in the face of violently hostile accusations: 'He was oppressed and afflicted, yet he did not open his mouth' (Isaiah 53:7). When falsely accused before the high priest he 'remained silent' (Matthew 26:63).

When Pilate himself questioned him, still 'Jesus made no reply, not even to a single charge' (Matthew 27:12-14). And even when King Herod got in on the act, eager for a prolonged interrogation, he 'gave him no answer' (Luke 23:9).

As someone once said, 'Never try to defend yourself – your real friends don't need it, and your enemies will never believe it!'

'No need to go overboard'

Nevertheless, in the face of so much opposition, there comes creeping into our room at night, or sometimes even in the bold light of day, the seductive temptation to *compromise.*

Seeing that we cannot be fully persuaded from our chosen course of action, some will try to weaken our determination just enough to make us accommodate their position in some form or another. Just as some members of Kenneth's church (we met him in chapter five) tried to persuade him to stay but not be so dogmatic about obedience to the Scriptures.

That was just the kind of subtle dealing Pharaoh attempted with Moses. God's desire has always been for a people liberated from slavery into a dimension of uninhibited worship of him. So, sending Moses to Pharaoh, the enslaver of his people, God's command was clear: 'Let my people go' (Exodus 8:1).

But Pharaoh hardened his heart towards the Lord and refused to allow the Israelites to leave the country. So the Lord sent a plague of water-to-blood, followed by plagues of frogs, gnats and flies, until Pharaoh, alerted by now to the power of the Lord, became eager for a settlement.

'Go, sacrifice to your God *here in the land*' (Exodus 8:25), he offered, thinking he could lure God into a compromise. But it was a totally unacceptable proposal.

Pharaoh had to learn, as must we all, that the will of God is not open to arbitration. You can accept it or you can reject it – but you can't change it!

The potentate of Egypt, however, hadn't learned that yet. Still thinking he could enter into political negotiation, just as he would with the petty monarchs of this world, Pharaoh put his next offer on the table: 'I will let you go to offer sacrifices to the Lord your God in the desert, *but you must not go very far'* (Exodus 8:28).

We cannot bargain with God this way. God wanted his people totally out of Egypt. And just to show who's boss, when the Israelites finally left, with Pharaoh's full consent, they didn't leave as paupers. They took with them great quantities of the gold and silver of Egypt, given to them freely by the people of the land!

Going to the other extreme

King Jeroboam, who led the rebellion of Israel against Judah after Solomon's death, used a similar ploy to secure his questionable rule over the newly-formed northern kingdom.

Under King David the centre for the worship of God had been established in Jerusalem, which was now in the southern kingdom of Judah, and Jeroboam realised the people would soon begin to question their allegiance to the north if they continued to make pilgrimage there. So, on the advice of his counsellors, he made two golden calves and, repeating the great sin of Israel in the wilderness, presented them as the gods that brought the people up from Egypt.

Setting up one in Bethel and the other in Dan, he put forward a compromised religion, saying, 'It is too much for you to go up to Jerusalem' (1 Kings 12:28).

Bethel (meaning 'House of God') had been the historic centre of worship before it was abandoned by God's choice of Jerusalem. So, cashing in on the strong emotional pulls of nostalgia, and seeking to rekindle allegiances of the past,

Jeroboam made a clever move.

Dan, however, was the most northerly town of the northern kingdom. It had no special religious significance and was about as far from Jerusalem as you could get! The chronicler records, 'This thing became a sin; the people went even as far as Dan to worship the [golden calf] there' (1 Kings 12:30).

It seems that when it has become too much to go God's way we open ourselves up, by way of compromise, to going right to the other extreme. If we give the devil an inch, he'll take a mile. And he'll keep on taking until suddenly we find ourselves miles from the original track.

Succumbing to compromise, we convince ourselves we have acted wisely. And we find some satisfaction in believing that, in view of the opposition, we have even performed the role of peacemaker. But in reality we have been lured into a fragile and deceptive armistice.

Are you prepared to obey *all* that the Lord has shown you?

13

Utter obedience

Jesus gave a clear and very sobering warning in his Sermon on the Mount: 'If. . . the light within you is darkness, how great is that darkness!' (Matthew 6:22).

We have all experienced the spiritual conflict that goes on in the heart and mind of a person who has seen something of God. Revelation has gripped our heart and we can no longer accept things as they are. There is something more, something better. Excitement begins to rise within us as we realise there is a call even upon *our* lives – even we have a destiny to fulfil.

Then the problems begin! Like the seed sown on rocky soil or among the thorns (Matthew 13:20-22), a conflict arises between the kingdom of God and the pressures of the world. If we aren't careful, compromise finds a place in us. Instead of a life filled with God and the truth of his Word, we can become clogged up with the cares of this world as it seeks to squeeze us back into its mould.

Often it creeps up on us unawares. We are halfway down that road before we realise what has happened. So how can we avoid getting into this situation? How can we ensure that the light within us remains light?

There is only one sure way, and it's costly: *complete and utter obedience to the Lord.*

'Where God wants me - job or no job'

The cost can take many forms, not least of which is a demand on our financial resources. It may be that to join those who are really moving with God demands a physical move. Just to be in the right church may mean leaving secure employment, a comfortable home or a pleasant location.

For Clifford it was all three. He had a prestigious and lucrative position in a company in Africa where he had worked for several years. Eventually, God called him and his wife Arlene to return to England. In obedience they returned, but it meant great upheaval and the financial costs were enormous. Leaving behind a large company house, servants, company cars and a huge salary - not to mention a very acceptable climate - they settled themselves in a small house in the Midlands and Clifford went back to university to do a further year's study.

They still had enough to live on, even though their income had dropped drastically. Clifford was unsure of what career move to make and, all in all, the first eighteen months were not easy. But they knew beyond the shadow of a doubt that they had done all God had asked of them - and believed he would honour their obedience.

They weren't disappointed. Not only did he bless the church through them, adding a whole new dimension of life to it as he used them in various forms of leadership, but he also provided for their needs over and above their expectations.

Clifford was offered an England-based position with the company he had worked for abroad. At first they wanted him to move to a city some eighty-five miles away, but Clifford was firm. 'This is where God has placed me, and this is where I'm staying,' he declared, 'job or no job.'

Stunned at his response, but eager to have him working for them again, the company contacted him a second time and reoffered him the job, this time allowing him to be based at his home!

Now, living in a beautiful house and financially stable again, he and Arlene are fulfilling in the church all that God has called them to at this time. They could have refused God's call to return to England, excusing their disobedience by reasoning that it was far too much to ask of anybody. But they didn't. They put God first, despite the financial cost, and in return God put them first every time.

'But what about my reputation?'

Then there is the cost in personal reputation. We are probably well received and widely accepted in our current church circle. If we change allegiance, all that will end. We will have to start all over again, unknown, unrecognised and laying down (initially, at least) any ministry we may have considered ours.

But what about our friends? They certainly won't understand, and probably won't be sympathetic – they haven't seen what we have seen. But we can't just ignore longstanding relationships, can we?

When God's call comes we must be prepared to lay all these things down. God is not sadistic. He's a loving God who only takes away in order to build up and strengthen his people, who will now be ready to receive from him in greater measure than before.

We have already met Bob (the former church deacon). His whole life was geared to becoming a full-time minister, until the day God broke in on him and radically changed his view of things. From that moment on, only one course of action was available to him. Compromise wasn't even considered. Laying down his ministry, and disregarding the incomprehension and bitterness of those left behind, he marched purposefully on into the will of God.

In his current leadership role, Bob is a strength to God's people in many ways. Leaving was a wrench at the time, but it was only a small price to pay for the 'greater thing' into which God was leading.

Such a person God can really take hold of and use. Such a person is open to the power of God's Spirit to shape and transform him.

It's not that he's perfect – he isn't. It's not that he found it easy to make his decision – he didn't. In fact, Bob had to call on God continually to strengthen him, show him the way through and enable him to deal with the antagonism. But through it all he was concerned with just one thing: doing what God wanted him to do.

That is all God asks of us.

The domino effect

Jesus urges us to count the cost. Financial cost, personal reputation, longstanding relationships – these are just some of the considerations. But the truth still stands that if we seek first the kingdom of God and his righteousness, all these things will be added to us anyway. We don't need to be worried about the whys and wherefores. All we need to do is be obedient to God and he'll take care of the rest.

Sadly, however, there are still some who seem to have more faith in the problem confronting them than in God's promise to supply all their needs. When the light within us begins to dim, we start making decisions based on the situation rather than on our revelation of God.

Imagine a person who has been introduced to a 'new' biblical truth – the baptism in the Holy Spirit, for example. With the eye of faith he sees and accepts his need for the Holy Spirit. He begins to reach out for it, but encounters opposition from the people in his local church. Captured by the call of God, he is all set to leave his church and join one where the baptism in the Holy Spirit is taught and practised.

Then comes the opposition. First from the few friends in whom he has excitedly confided, then from the minister himself, who has personally rejected the Holy Spirit. Warnings range from 'the work of the devil' to 'it's a thing of the past, not valid today'. As he allows the pressures to intrude on his thinking his original faith begins to waver.

The once radiant beams of inspiration begin to fade. As more obstacles begin to present themselves, clouds of uncertainty start to roll in and he begins to fear the cost of embracing this new-found truth.

The new church is twenty miles away – costly in terms of time and money. And he knows no-one there very well, while at his current church he has close friends and is respected as a man of some standing. Does he really want to give it all up?

As this destructive pattern of thought continues, the long shadows of doubt are almost welcome as they conspire to convince him that he is doing rather well where he is. Does he really need to get himself involved with this dodgy idea? The black night of unbelief finally overtakes him as he settles back into the darkness of disobedience to God's once clear call to move on.

The light that was in him has become darkness – and how dark it has become! No longer motivated by what he once saw, he can now only justify his position by opposing it. Not entering in himself, he is a hindrance to those who would enter (Luke 11:52).

Not a pleasant picture, and perhaps a bit far-fetched, you may say. But it happens! How easily we allow the problem, rather than God, to rule our thinking. Once we allow it to dominate us, the domino effect takes over and one thing topples after another.

Don't fool yourself

The apostle Paul once confronted the Galatian Christians. The converts from his ministry in Galatia had begun well in the dynamism of the Holy Spirit but were now succumbing to pressure from proselytising legalists. Dead religious form was threatening to stifle the living, righteous freedom which Jesus had won.

To Paul, this was falling from grace, moving into deception – an act of desperate foolishness. 'You foolish Galatians! Who has bewitched you?' he cried (Galatians 3:1).

Having been liberated by Jesus they were again subjecting themselves to the yoke of bondage. They were going back into what they had come out of. And Paul did not baulk at describing what that would mean from his point of view: 'If I rebuild what I destroyed, I prove that I am a law-breaker' (Galatians 2:18).

When we are diverted from the highway of God's purpose back into the byway from which we came, we are in danger. Throwing our energies back into what we once determined to forsake is not just inconsistent but unrighteous. We prove ourselves to be transgressors. We may throw ourselves back into the old ways with renewed dedication. We may work with determined energy. But in the end it is nothing more than the outworking of a deep-rooted desperation.

We are fooling ourselves – and in the quiet moments, if we are honest, we know it. We know that we are trying to make something work that we have no real faith to see succeed. And the Word of God confronts us with: 'Everything that does not come from faith is sin' (Romans 14:23).

Maybe we do believe on a good day – when the sun is shining, the wind is in the right direction and everything in the garden looks lovely. Perhaps it's only on the bad days, when we've had to take off our rose-tinted spectacles, that our despair gives way to depression.

But Scripture has a word for the person in that condition. He is called 'double-minded . . . unstable in all he does'. The only thing he can be sure of is that he won't receive anything from the Lord (James 1:6-7).

So don't fool yourself. If you can't proceed down that road in faith, heed the 'No Entry' signs. Instead, go where faith draws you. Follow hard where it can flourish. And don't even begin to think, 'Yes, I know I should, but . . .' The Word of God says:

'My righteous one will live by faith. And if he shrinks back, I will not be pleased with him' (Hebrews 10:38).

Again, the sharp two-edged sword of the Word cuts through the thoughts and intentions of our hearts, leaving us exposed and without excuse, when it states: 'To the one who knows the right thing to do, and does not do it, to him it is sin' (James 4:17 NASB).

One excuse after another

Teresa knew 'the right thing to do' but she put forward one excuse after another to avoid doing it.

Raised a Roman Catholic, she had attended a Catholic church for thirty-six years before she came to know Jesus personally. Not long after, she received the baptism in the Holy Spirit. Through her involvement with a prayer group, with a community specialising in the healing ministry and with a woman from another church who became a close friend, her spiritual growth was rapid. She attended her friend's church on several occasions and eventually God asked her to move there permanently.

'I was more and more dissatisfied and unhappy at my old church,' she related. 'Not many were interested in moving on with God. It had become so unreal compared to what I'd been experiencing, and I'd begun to question the reality of what was happening there. Even so, the decision was a difficult one to make. I had been so much a Catholic, and I raised before God every argument possible for staying where I was.

' "It wouldn't be fair on my father," I thought. He had just moved to be near us because of his health, and went to church with me every week. "The children won't like it. The new church is fifteen miles away and my husband won't stand for it. I won't fit in at the new place – I'm not the right sort of person. And if I stay where I am I can have an effect for God on the people I see every Sunday."

'But none of my arguments held water in the light of what

I knew God was saying, and he gently but firmly showed me I was wrong.

'God immediately provided my father with an alternative lift to church and now his faith is becoming real and alive. The children, now they have settled, love it – and the teaching they are getting is practical and relevant.

'To my absolute amazement, my non-Christian husband approved of the change, even though the Sunday meeting meant spending a whole morning away from home instead of just an hour. And I realised that I did fit in at the new church. My friend had moved away by this time, which was sad, but there was so much love for me there, and acceptance of me for who I was, that I really felt I'd come home.

'As for staying put to be a light in my old church, I soon saw that most of them didn't want to change at all. I've had more effect on people who don't know God at all than I've had on them.'

Fortunately for Teresa, she didn't allow the doubts to obscure what she had seen. Yes, there had been resistance, the circumstances conspiring to dissuade her from obeying God. But as she remained open to the Lord, he showed her the way through each apparent obstacle.

Her final comment? 'Don't be afraid. The devil's lies are powerful, but don't let him stop you coming into a Spirit-filled church and reaching for the abundance of all that God has for you. Had I known then what I know now, I would never have hesitated.'

Prize or compromise?

What I have tried to do in these last two chapters is dispel the false and dangerous reasoning that compromise is a godly solution. Once and for all I want to pull down the idea that in the kingdom of God it is legitimate to go for the soft option or take the attitude of 'Anything for the sake of a quiet life'.

Compromising over convictions implanted in you by the Holy

Spirit and accommodating ideas contrary to God's Word is nothing less than bad, old-fashioned *sin.* Not only is it ungodly – it is downright dangerous. Such active disobedience to God will, in the end, disqualify you from receiving all that could have been yours by way of eternal reward.

Closely linked with compromise is negligence, another subtle robber of reward, and just as big an enemy to destiny as disobedience. Remember, it was to the church, not the world, that the warning was addressed: 'How shall we escape if we neglect so great a salvation?' (Hebrews 2:3 NASB).

You may not be neglecting the wonderful fact that you are saved, but are you neglecting the greatness of the salvation into which you have come?

Don't be content with less than all God has for you. There may be a great price to pay – but there is a glorious prize to win!

14

Reward and prize – gain or loss?

A notoriously emotional member of the congregation approached the pastor after an evidently inspired sermon.

'Oh pastor, your message really moved me this morning,' was the effusive compliment, accompanied by copious tears.

'Good,' replied the man of God, '– where to?'

The word of God always demands a response. It comes to produce not just feelings but faith leading to action. But we are all prone to be carried away by emotion. Perhaps there has been a television appeal for aid following a recent disaster. Stirred to compassion by the grim pictures of people who have lost everything – home, business, maybe even family – we determine to give generously.

If we don't really have the means at the time, we decide, after the first rush of enthusiasm, to wait until we next get paid. But by that time, although we still feel sorry for the people involved, our compassion has cooled. Either we send less than we originally intended or, more likely, we send nothing at all. After all, we reason, we have our own needs to consider, and so many others are sending money that our little contribution won't make much difference anyway.

What has happened? What we saw stirred an emotional response but the image wasn't sufficient, or sustained long enough, to produce action.

That is what often happens with the word of God. We read it, or we hear it, and we receive it gladly, marvelling at its wisdom and its potential for success if applied in our lives. But, as with the seed sown on rocky places or among thorns, we quickly forget about it. We allow the cares of the world to take priority, never giving it a chance to take root within us (see Mark 4). What had once so gripped us has now been lost.

It is vital, therefore, that the word we hear or read be allowed to move us to *action.* When it does, there are great benefits to be reaped.

King David focuses our attention on two opposite motivational forces of God's commands: 'By them is your servant warned; in keeping them there is great reward' (Psalm 19:11).

God's Word gives *warnings* to prevent us from rambling the wrong way, but at the same time offers *rewards* to propel us into running the right way.

Reward is a motivation

This is where many of us have to change our thinking. The idea of actually being rewarded for our faithfulness is by and large foreign to evangelical believers. It smacks of 'salvation by works', which is anathema to us all.

But that isn't what God has in mind. True, once we are saved, we are saved, and that's it – just as being our parents' child is a biological fact which nothing can ever change. It is a gift of God's grace. But once saved, we have a choice to make. We can try to ignore the fact and carry on much as we did before, settling for a half-hearted, compromised sort of Christianity which never requires a move out of the comfort zone. Or we can decide to go one hundred percent for God, abandoning ourselves to him completely. Reward is one significant motivation to choose the latter.

Using the imagery of the athlete and the winner's prize, the Bible shows us that reward has been a strong motivating factor in the life of all the great servants of God – and that it should be in ours, too.

The writer to the Hebrews urges us to 'run with perseverance the race marked out for us', looking to Jesus, our example, who, 'for the joy set before him', was able to endure the horrors of the cross and win (Hebrews 12:1-2). Paul reminds Timothy that 'if anyone competes as an athlete, he does not receive the victor's crown unless he competes according to the rules' (2 Timothy 2:5). And he encourages the church at Corinth to 'run in such a way as to get the prize' (1 Corinthians 9:24).

The apostle himself lived in the light of that prize, boldly practising what he preached. 'I press on towards the goal,' he stated, 'to win the prize for which God has called me heavenwards in Christ Jesus' (Philippians 3:14).

To that end, Paul kept himself under a strict regime of godly discipline, constantly bringing himself into submission to the purposes of God, 'so that after I have preached to others, I myself will not be disqualified for the prize' (1 Corinthians 9:27).

He wasn't afraid of losing his salvation, but he was conscious that he could lose his prize.

Watch over yourselves

The weeks before exam time are always critical. We study and sweat, and we study some more, and if we haven't done much work through the year, late nights and bleary eyes become a regular feature.

There are a few who sail through their exams and, with no apparent effort, get a grade 'A' every time. But for most of us it means a lot of hard work. Yet it's worth it. What a shame it would be if we were to throw away all the years of school or college which have led up to this, simply because we weren't willing to put in the time, discipline and hard work when it was needed.

Why risk getting only a grade 'E' when you could achieve a grade 'B' or higher? And why increase the pressure upon yourself at exam time by failing to work diligently throughout the year? Rushing around copying other people's notes from lectures you failed to attend and had totally forgotten about until now does nothing either for your confidence or your prospects.

Or look at it in terms of your employment. You have ability, drive and experience. Success in your job will mean promotion opportunities, handsome increases in your salary and generous year-end bonuses. Not to mention a company car and regular business trips abroad.

If that's what you want you won't turn up late for work every morning, shout at the boss and go all-out to lose the company valuable contracts, will you? No! You'll work long and hard to achieve your goal. Like Paul, you'll run the race to win.

That is exactly how it should be in the kingdom of God. Once we are convinced that there is a race to run and a glorious prize to win, we should be running diligently. Like Paul, we will discipline ourselves so that, having started out well, there may be no reason to be disqualified later on.

Disqualification is possible. One fails his exams through lack of study. Another fails to get his promotion through lack of diligence. And, spiritually speaking, we can nullify what we have achieved in the past by our actions today.

'Watch out,' warned John, 'that you do not lose what you have worked for, but that you may be rewarded fully' (2 John 8). And Jesus urged, 'Hold on to what you have, so that no-one will take your crown' (Revelation 3:11).

So let's heed the warning and be like Paul who, when his earthly life was reaching its end, was confident he had made it – he had won! 'I have finished the race, I have kept the faith. Now there is in store for me the crown of righteousness, which the Lord, the righteous Judge, will award to me on that day' (2 Timothy 4:7-8).

For those who seek him earnestly

Let's be clear, however, about the attitude we should be taking towards this reward issue. The great pull on our hearts of the expectation of reward should not be a worldly, carnal matter. If we are genuine Christians we will not be going after God simply for what we can get; it will be a fundamental part of our relationship with him.

The writer to the Hebrews tells us that 'without faith it is impossible to please God, because anyone who comes to him must believe that he exists and that he rewards those who earnestly seek him' (Hebrews 11:6). There is nothing wrong in going for the reward but, in doing so, we must be earnestly seeking God.

Abraham continued faithfully in his pilgrimage, and in his utter dependence upon God, spurred on by the promise of a 'very great reward' (Genesis 15:1).

Moses gave up position, prestige, possessions and pleasures to take his stand with the people of God. Refusing the natural, he chose the spiritual. Weighing up the options – treasures of Egypt or reproach of Christ – he concluded that commitment to the purposes of God was worth far more than any comfort in the palace of Pharaoh, 'because he was looking ahead to his reward' (Hebrews 11:24-26).

As for us, the choices we make, the lifestyle we embrace and the ministry we undertake all contribute to the prize we win. We will be rewarded not only for the way we have lived, but also for the work we have done: 'Each will be rewarded according to his own labour' (1 Corinthians 3:8). So it is vitally important that we build the right way. It's not a question of 'Will I be lost?' but of 'Will I suffer loss?'

All this is vitally relevant to the church loyalty question. How can I reconcile going for the prize with a local church life which is hidebound and restrictive? I want fellow-Christians in my church to be cheering me on in the race, not trying to trip me up or, at best, shouting, 'Slow down a bit!'

'Each man must be careful how he builds'

Urging the Corinthians to build correctly on the foundation of Jesus Christ, Paul said: 'If any man's work which he has built upon it remains, he shall receive a reward. If any man's work is burned up, he shall suffer loss; but he himself shall be saved' (1 Corinthians 3:10, 14-15 NASB).

Just as disastrous as working hard, only to let it all go at the end and losing our reward, is putting our life's energies into constructing a building that is destined only to be burned up. How tragic if, after having a lifetime to accumulate treasure in heaven, we eventually stand before the Lord with no reward.

It's like the do-it-yourself man who invested a lot of time and effort in building a home extension only to watch it gradually fall apart because he had built it the wrong way.

The Lord may be a rewarder of those who earnestly seek him, but *he isn't necessarily a rewarder of those who attempt to serve him without first enquiring how or where to serve him.* Our number one responsibility is to seek the Lord in faith, expecting him to direct us into ways of profitable service and successful work.

We only have one life to live, and one life to give. We must redeem the time while it is today so as to qualify to reap the rewards in eternity. For when the Lord comes he will bring the rewards with him (see Isaiah 40:10; 62:11; Revelation 22:12).

Whatever you do, don't give up in despair and write yourself off as just another also-ran in the race to fulfil God's purpose in your life and generation. It may seem like an impossible task. The warnings may sound rather intimidating, and you may feel that you have failed so many times in the past. But all you need to do is keep your eyes fixed on Jesus – and determine to walk in faith and obedience only to him.

He doesn't intend us to fail. He intends us to succeed, and in our times of weakness he has all the strength we need.

And be encouraged by the fact that this is a unique race in that there isn't just one winner. In the race set before us, *all* can win, not just Abraham and Moses, apostles and prophets and other prominent Christians.

The Word of God describes a great presentation day that is coming, a prize-giving jubilee that will shame the piffling ceremonies and perishable crowns of this world into utter insignificance. Yes, kings will be there. And yes, there will be prophets, apostles and all the great and mighty men and women of God. But right there, among all the greats, will also be the small – you and me. We too have our indispensable part to play, and our individual prize to win (Revelation 11:18).

Reward and prize – gain or loss? It's up to you. Can you allow *anything,* least of all a misplaced local church loyalty, to hold you back?

15

A tale of two cities

The battle that rages between good and evil, God and the devil, has long held people fascinated. This great spiritual conflict has inspired many an epic writer to tales of heroism and adventure, and people have used all kinds of imagery to depict the continuing struggle.

The Bible has its own ways of illustrating the war between the spiritual and the carnal, the righteous and the unrighteous, but one in particular stands out. From Genesis to Revelation it speaks of the historic conflict of two great cities: Zion, the holy city of God, and Babylon, the godless city of man.

The first hint of Babylon, in Genesis 11, shows the carnal nature of this man-centred place. The inhabitants of the post-flood world, unwilling to learn the lessons of the past, determined to build for themselves 'a city, and a tower whose top will reach into heaven' and, by so doing, make a name for themselves (Genesis 11:4 NASB). They laboured hard, manufacturing bricks in an arrogant attempt to reach up to the heights of heaven by the achievement of their own hands.

By contrast, the same chapter also provides us with the first hint of Zion, the city of God.

Here we find Abraham (still known as Abram) and his family setting out on a pilgrimage 'from Ur of the Chaldeans to go to Canaan' (Genesis 11:31). The Lord had appeared to Abraham before the journey began (Acts 7:2) and, commanding him to leave his country and his people for a land he would show him, motivated him by a vision of the holy city (Hebrews 11:10).

Unlike Babel, the city Abraham looked for had eternal foundations. It had been designed and built by God himself. In utter contrast to the unsuccessful attempt of the Babel builders to elevate themselves from the earth to the heavens, Zion, the holy city, the heavenly Jerusalem, is 'coming down *out of* heaven from God' (Revelation 21:10).

The two cities are totally incompatible. They are built on different foundations, to a different construction and by a different motivation. And they are continually at enmity. Babylon prides itself in the pursuit of humanistic philosophy, where men and women are the authors of their own salvation. Full of the carnality of the world, there is no room for God. She is a harlot city reserved for ultimate destruction (see Revelation 18).

Zion, on the other hand, the bride of Christ and totally God-centred, shines 'with the glory of God' and is destined for eternal blessing (Revelation 21:11).

Which city are you building?

Every man or woman who ever lived participates in the construction of one or other of these cities. Either they are building the kingdom of God and are destined for that holy city, or they are busy placing futile stone upon futile stone of that man-made edifice that is so taken up with the world that it has no room for God.

In case you think I'm being dogmatic in insisting that everyone is building in either of these two places, let me remind you that Jesus said: 'He who is not with me is against me, and he who does not gather with me scatters' (Matthew 12:30). If we are not building the kingdom of God then, unwittingly or not and whether we like it or not, we are serving the devil's purposes.

Here is the great subtlety and deception of the devil: although, spiritually, the virgin bride and the vulgar harlot are worlds apart, superficially they are similar. The devil isn't stupid. He knows that the counterfeit only has the ability to succeed because of its likeness to the original, and he has gone to great lengths to provide some very convincing counterfeits.

Ferocious wolves, seeking to destroy the flock of God, first adorn themselves with sheepskins. The false prophet in the book of Revelation might speak like a dragon, but he looks like a lamb. And many, with much enthusiasm and little knowledge, have happily accepted the counterfeit, mistaking it for the real.

Katrina, not having read the warning in Deuteronomy 18:10-12, was not aware that in attending a spiritualist 'church' she was settling herself on the devil's territory. She was involved with it for a whole year before realising that what went on there was not of God but devil-inspired. Three years on, now born again and baptised in the Holy Spirit, she sees the situation clearly:

'They claimed to be Christians,' she remembered. 'They sang hymns, said the Lord's Prayer, had Bible readings. And I even saw them exercise gifts similar to those given by the Holy Spirit and listed in 1 Corinthians 12.

'On the surface everything looked right, but in reality everything was wrong. There was no genuine love in that place. They didn't know Jesus personally – though some claimed to. God was just a far-off, untouchable being to them, and no lasting comfort came from their devil-inspired, so-called messages from the dead.

'The whole place stank of death. It's just that, at first, not having experienced the reality of Jesus for myself, I was deceived, and couldn't sense it.'

It's easy to fall into the trap. The devil knows how to counterfeit the real and we must be on the alert. Not just people in Katrina's situation – which you may argue is an extreme case – but every one of us could be fooled. Right now, many of God's genuine people who are working hard in what they would call 'proper' churches, believing themselves to be building the kingdom of God, are in fact resident in a Babylon they have either built with their own hands or have allowed to be built up around them.

Babylon, you see, isn't just some weird cult or obviously demonic religious set-up. It is *everything that is not of the kingdom of God.* It is *everything that is at variance with what God has said in his Word* – whether it be someone trying to contact the dead through a medium or someone wanting to walk in the ways of God but unwilling to embrace some part of God's Word which makes him feel uncomfortable.

If we try to exclude God in any way, we are no longer looking for the holy city. As we revert to trying to build in our own way (like our original do-it-yourself man), Babylon's bricks are already in our hand.

We can call it Babel, Sodom, Egypt or even 'the present city of Jerusalem' and we would still be talking about the same thing (Galatians 4:25). It is man-made effort that contrasts with the God-given access into the heavens (see Genesis 28:10-17; John 1:51). Remember, 'our God is a consuming fire' and what we have spent our lives building will be tested by the fire of God himself (1 Corinthians 3:12-15).

According to the writer to the Hebrews, there is a great shaking coming, one destined to remove everything that can be shaken so that, ultimately, only the unshakable kingdom of God will remain.

As Christians we have come to Mount Zion, he tells us, 'to the heavenly Jerusalem, the city of the living God'. And he warns those whose names are written in the Lamb's book of life, yet are still fellowshipping with spiritual death in Babylon, not to refuse God but to give heed to the warning from heaven (Hebrews 12:22-29).

The call from the Lord is clear: 'Come out of her, my people, so that you will not share in her sins, so that you will not receive any of her plagues; for her sins are piled up to heaven, and God has remembered her crimes' (Revelation 18:4-5).

Help or hindrance?

It is time for God's unshakable kingdom to become evident. It is time for the real church to emerge, built faithfully to scriptural patterns, moving steadily on in God's purposes and consisting exclusively of people born again by the Spirit of God.

The hastening or hindering of its emergence is very largely in our hands. We have a hand in eternal affairs.

Not only are we to 'look forward' to the day of Jesus' return but, by the determined action of lives lived by faith in the light of God's ultimate intention, we can even 'speed its coming' (2 Peter 3:10-12). It is to this that we are called.

But just as faithfulness and obedience will bring us into the fulness of God's purposes, unbelief and disobedience will disqualify us from them.

When Abraham began his journey from Ur it was in the company of his father Terah. Together they headed for Canaan, but when they arrived in Haran they stayed there until Terah died, after which the call of God came to Abraham again. The call was the same. God's purpose was unchanged. But one generation had missed its opportunity.

Abraham's nephew, Lot, at first moved on with his uncle. But he was motivated more by desire than destiny. Lifting up his eyes and seeing the well-watered valley of the Jordan, like the garden of the Lord and like Egypt, he chose to go that way. God commanded Abraham, however, to lift up his eyes and look north, south, east and west and behold the land of his inheritance (Genesis 13:10-18).

Lot saw his immediate comfort, but Abraham received his ultimate call.

It isn't surprising, then, that we soon discover Lot living in corrupt Sodom. And although his righteous soul was tormented day after day by the lawless deeds of its inhabitants, he made no attempt to remove himself from among them. God's judgment, however, had already been passed on Sodom, a city lacking even ten righteous citizens, and the angels of the Lord were sent to rescue Lot by warning him of the coming wrath and commanding him to flee to the mountains. To remain would be fatal, for by remaining he would be participating in her sins and, as a result, would 'receive of her plagues'.

Despite such desperate urgency, Lot hesitated until the angels had to physically pull him out of the city. And even then he continued to argue and seek a compromise so as not to have to go all the way to the mountains! But God, in his loving patience and mercy, not being willing for any innocent person to suffer, held back his judgment until Lot and his family were out of the condemned city (Genesis 19).

How many Lots are there today, I wonder, who are holding back the righteous judgments of the Lord - judgments that further the purposes of God and reveal his holiness - simply because they refuse to obey his voice and dissociate themselves from his enemies? How many creaking and mixturised denominations litter Christendom today because God's redeemed people within them refuse to budge? Only when they make their exits can God's righteous judgments clear the scene to make room for something better - a church worth the name.

Or how many who purport to be building the kingdom of God and hastening the day of the Lord's coming are, in reality, a hindrance to his work?

Looking back over the testimonies in this book, it's easy to conclude that it's not a small number. But don't despair. We may not be able to do anything about them but we can do something about ourselves.

Make your time count for eternity

Lot's rescue was undertaken because the Lord 'remembered Abraham' (Genesis 19:29). It was on the same grounds that he was later moved to deliver Israel from Egypt (Exodus 2:24-25). He remembered his covenant with Abraham and so brought the children of Abraham out of the land of pressure into the land of promise.

During their journey through the desert he taught them that 'man does not live on bread alone but on every word that comes from the mouth of the Lord' (Deuteronomy 8:3). But the message they heard was of no value to them because those who heard it did not combine it with faith. Those who had had the good news preached to them failed to enter the promised land because of their disobedience (Hebrews 4:2, 6).

An entire generation perished in the wilderness, having witnessed at first hand the *works* of God, but remaining ignorant of his *ways* (Psalm 103:7).

Today it is we Christians, the body of Christ, who are the children of Abraham and the inheritors of the promise (Romans 4). Like our predecessors, we have a destiny to fulfil and an inheritance to claim.

So let's get on with it. We can't afford to waste another generation. For, however many generations are to come, one thing is sure: we won't get another shot at the target. This is the final generation *for us.*

There is a church to build, a world to save and a kingdom to usher in. It is for this that we were redeemed, for this that we have become responsible – and for this that we will be rewarded. So let's not delay. Dare to believe it. Dare to act on it.

Make your time count for eternity!

Appendix

Some useful practical points

The fundamentals

Readers from certain church backgrounds may have been puzzled about some of the terms used in this book, such as 'born again' and 'baptised in the Holy Spirit'. These are basic to biblical Christianity and it has been taken for granted that they have been understood and, hopefully, experienced.

If you are puzzled and wish to know more, I recommend *Belonging* by David Matthew (Harvestime). Subtitled *Local church membership,* this little book gives a simple outline of what it means to become a Christian and become part of a live local church.

Checking your motives

You may be tempted to leave a church for dubious motives. Check that none of the following is true of you:

☐ you are basically a wanderer and fancy another change

☐ you are angry because someone else was given a position of responsibility which you felt you deserved

☐ you have had a difference of opinion with someone in the church and find it easier to move churches than to resolve the issue in a biblical manner

☐ one of the leaders has confronted you over a personal fault or weakness and you are unwilling to face up to it

What, then, could be considered valid reasons for making a move? I suggest any of the following:

☐ the leader is not born again. The Lord doesn't place his 'sheep' under the care of 'goats'

☐ the Bible is not recognised as the Word of God, so robbing you of any objective standard for Christian practice

☐ unbelievers are accepted into membership

☐ baptism of believers in water is not practised

☐ the baptism and gifts of the Holy Spirit are denied as valid for today and their practice is attributed either to mere psychological factors or to demons

☐ sin and unrighteousness in church members are allowed to continue unchallenged by the leadership

☐ the church and its programme lacks a prophetic element, maintaining routines rather than moving forward consistently in the life of God

☐ despite your own efforts, the church is not helping you to grow and make progress in spiritual life and maturity

☐ there is tension, bickering, strife and party-spirit

Making the move

If the time comes when you know you must leave your church, it is vital to do so with courtesy and integrity.

Don't just disappear or give a false reason for leaving. For instance, 'We feel we should transfer to such-and-such a church because their meeting-place is much nearer to our home' could be misleading. The statement about distances may be true, but is that the *real* reason for moving?

Normally, it is best to arrange to see the minister or pastor face to face and explain with complete honesty your reasons for leaving. If it is a 'shake the dust off your feet' situation, be firm yet gracious, avoiding a 'holier than thou' attitude. He may well put pressure on you to reconsider, so be absolutely clear of the way forward before you meet him.

In some circumstances a clearly-written letter would suffice, but a face-to-face statement is nearly always best.

Be sure that you have handed over in a tidy and satisfactory form any responsibilities that your leaving will require you to relinquish.

Be sure, too, that you have looked beyond the moving out to what you are moving *into*. One thing is clear: there is absolutely no biblical justification for staying unattached, or for being a wanderer who drops in on meetings at a variety of churches without putting down roots in any of them.

What is God saying?

God speaks to us on this whole subject in different ways. On a general level, he gives in his Word clear principles of association, which this book has attempted to outline. He expects us to apply these principles to our own situation with spiritual common sense and act accordingly. There will be no need to seek God in prayer for further indications of his will.

Some situations, however, are less clear-cut, and this is where, in addition to applying these principles in a general way, you will need to have a clear directive from the Lord as to whether you should stay or move. This may come through a growing inner conviction as you spend time in prayer; through a clear prompting of the Holy Spirit; or through a prophetic word (but beware of *unchecked* directive prophecy of a personal nature).

By all means talk to other Christians about your situation, but bear in mind that their advice may be coloured by vested interest or motivation which is not true to the Word of God. In the final analysis you must stay or move out of deep personal conviction, not because of what someone else has said.

'God is not a God of disorder but of peace' (1 Corinthians 14:33). He will not leave you in confusion over this important issue if you are genuine in your desire to know his will.